# REBUILDING
## THE
# WALL

Restoring our broken lives through the book of Nehemiah

## BY SUSAN MATHIS

Copyright © 2024 Susan Mathis

All rights reserved. This book or any portion thereof may not be reproduced or used in any manner whatsoever without the express written permission of the publisher except for the use of brief quotations in a book review.

Scriptures marked NLT are taken from The Holy Bible, New Living Translation, copyright © 1996, 2004, 2015 by Tyndale House Foundation. Used by permission of Tyndale House Publishers, Inc., Carol Stream, Illinois 60188. All rights reserved.

Scriptures marked NIV are taken from the Holy Bible, New International Version®, NIV®. Copyright © 1973, 1978, 1984, 2011 by Biblica, Inc.™ Used by permission of Zondervan.

Default Bible version NKJV

First printing 2024 in the United States of America

ISBN: 979-8-218-40444-4

The ideas or suggestions presented in this book are intended for informational purposes only and should not be considered a substitute for professional counseling or therapy. Every individual's circumstances are unique, and what works for one person may not be suitable for another. It is strongly recommended to seek guidance from qualified professionals for personalized support tailored to your specific needs. The author and publisher disclaim any liability arising directly or indirectly from the use of the information provided in this book.

# DEDICATION

With deep gratitude, I dedicate this book to the guiding presence of the Holy Spirit, whose inspiration flowed through me as I penned these words.

To my cherished son, your unwavering encouragement spurred me on; to my beloved daughter, for your help; to my devoted husband, whose meticulous hours of reading and editing refined these pages. And to my dear granddaughter, your uplifting words fueled my persistence; this journey might have faltered without you.

With love and appreciation, this work is forever devoted to each of you.

# CONTENTS

Jericho Walls ........................................ 6

Introduction ........................................ 7

Chapter 1 The Sheep Gate ........................ 13

Chapter 2 The Fish Gate .......................... 21

Chapter 3 The Old Gate ........................... 32

Chapter 4 The Valley Gate ....................... 46

Chapter 5 The Refuse Gate ....................... 55

Chapter 6 Summary of the First Five Gates ...... 63

Chapter 7 The Fountain Gate ..................... 67

Chapter 8 The Water Gate ........................ 83

Chapter 9 The Horse Gate ........................ 92

Chapter 10 The East Gate ........................ 112

Chapter 11 The Inspection Gate .................. 121

Chapter 12 So I'm Restored Now, Right? ......... 132

Review of the Walls and Gates ..................... 139

Map of the Walls and Gates....................... 143

About the Author................................ 145

# JERICHO WALLS

"Next to Eliashib the men of Jericho built"
Nehemiah 3:2.

The ancient walls of Jericho that had been an obstacle to the Israelites had fallen long ago. Much later, the Babylonians came in and destroyed Jerusalem with its wall. Although the people had rebuilt the temple, the wall remained in ruins.

Now, under the guidance of Nehemiah, the people were rebuilding that wall —and even a few men from Jericho were helping.

We often construct unhealthy Jericho walls around ourselves to protect us, but sometimes, these barriers can isolate us from others and even from God. It's essential to break down these self-made defenses and build healthier Nehemiah walls, the walls God meant us to have.

# INTRODUCTION

Wall: A high, thick masonry structure forming a long rampart or an enclosure chiefly for defense
-Merriam Webster Dictionary, 1997

The book of Nehemiah has been an inspiration to me as a crucial part of God's Word. Although you might have read it, you may have wondered why building walls is significant and why the Bible details it so thoroughly. I believe that every book of the Bible has a purpose and importance that we can apply to our lives.

"All Scripture is given by inspiration of God, and is profitable for doctrine, for reproof, for correction, for instruction in righteousness." 2 Timothy 3:16

As I reflect on my own experiences and struggles in life, I can see how the story about Nehemiah's rebuilding of the wall of Jerusalem can be applied to our own lives. Just as Nehemiah faced opposition and challenges, we also will encounter obstacles and difficulties in our lives. But just as Nehemiah remained steadfast in his faith and determination to complete the task set before him, we, too, can find strength through Christ to persevere through our struggles.

The book of Nehemiah serves as a reminder of the significance of believers who work together towards a common goal of serving Christ. Nehemiah alone couldn't have rebuilt the wall, and it was only through the collaboration and dedication of the people that the project was accomplished.

Likewise, we should acknowledge the importance of others in the body of Christ. Overall, the book of Nehemiah is a testament to the power of faith, perseverance, and family. It reminds us that no matter how challenging our circumstances may be, we can still find hope and strength in God's Word and the support of those around us.

As we draw inspiration from Nehemiah's steadfast faith and the collaborative effort of the people in rebuilding the wall of Jerusalem, it may be helpful to understand some historical background that set the stage for these events. The Babylonians had destroyed Jerusalem, the temple, and its wall around it, and had taken many people into exile.

Years later, Zerubbabel returned with a large group to rebuild the temple, and approximately fifty years after that, Ezra arrived with more followers. A dedicated scribe, Ezra focused on learning and teaching the law of Moses. Despite these efforts, the wall around Jerusalem remained in ruin.

We know that solid walls and a sturdy door are crucial to protect us from unwanted intruders. However, we may also create emotional walls that keep us from meaningful connections with others. These invisible walls act as barriers that shield us from potential harm and hurt.

Sometimes, we erect walls of unforgiveness, past offenses, or bitterness that stop us from being open and honest with others. While we may feel safe behind these walls, we may also isolate ourselves from those who care about us. It can be difficult to share our emotions and how we feel with others when we have emotional pain. To be cautious and hesitant is natural, but we should remember that building walls around ourselves may not always be the best solution.

As we contemplate the impact of emotional walls in our lives, it's intriguing to see a parallel in the ancient words of Nehemiah, who, faced with the literal broken walls of Jerusalem, sought to understand the condition of his people. Just as the physical walls were in disrepair, so too can emotional barriers hinder our connections with others.

The words of Nehemiah the son of Hachaliah:

"It came to pass in the month of Chislev, in the twentieth year, as I was in Shushan the citadel, that Hanani one of my brethren came with men from Judah; and I asked them concerning the Jews who had escaped, who had survived the captivity, and concerning Jerusalem. And they said to me, 'The survivors who are left from the captivity in the province are there in great distress and reproach. The wall of Jerusalem is also broken down, and its gates are burned with fire" Nehemiah 1:1-3.

Ezra had arrived in Jerusalem several years earlier. Now Nehemiah longed to know how the work was progressing. He saw some brethren who had come from there, so he asked them how things were. The temple had been rebuilt, and Ezra was teaching them about the law of Moses. So no more needed to be done, right? After all, the people had a place of worship again.

Instead, however, Nehemiah received some worrisome news from his brethren. They informed him that the people were in great distress as the wall lay destroyed and the gates had been burned with fire. This incident shows that while we may appear to be strong and resilient on the outside, we could be emotionally vulnerable and unprotected on the inside.

Our bodies and souls are like temples, and just like walls

around a physical temple, our emotional walls could lie broken down, leaving us exposed and defenseless.

What was Nehemiah's reaction to this news?

"So it was, when I heard these words, that I sat down and wept, and mourned for many days; I was fasting and praying before the God of heaven" Nehemiah 1:4. He sat down, and he wept and mourned for days. It is worth considering whether Nehemiah's grief for the people's affliction is relevant to our contemporary lives. The name *Nehemiah* means God comforts, and Nehemiah represents the Holy Spirit.

When our lives are shattered and filled with pain, we can turn to our heavenly Father for comfort. He understands and grieves with us and takes our wounds and broken, charred lives to heart. He is deeply concerned about our emotional and mental health. He knows the more we receive reconstruction in these areas, the stronger our spiritual relationship with Him will become.

Walls built in the world have different uses. Some are for protection to keep enemies out, or we can use walls for decorative purposes. I see two kinds of walls in the Bible: Jericho walls and Nehemiah walls. The Jericho walls represent unhealthy emotional walls. We build these broken boundaries to keep ourselves safe from the hurts and pain of the past and future.

Everyone has unique emotional barriers, some of which can harm their well-being. Emotional walls can take many forms. Suppressing emotions to avoid extreme joy or sadness, fear of rejection, low self-esteem, resistance to change, pride, and stubbornness are just a few examples. There are also many other types of emotional walls that people might experience.

We think these walls protect us; however, these walls must

come down. The Nehemiah walls stand for healthy emotional and spiritual boundaries. These are the walls God created for us to have. But these Nehemiah walls, now broken and shattered through life's trials and emotional pain, lie just inside the Jericho walls we have built.

Our Nehemiah walls are in desperate need of repair and rebuilding. As we rebuild the Nehemiah walls, we construct better emotional boundaries, which will, a little at a time, demolish the unhealthy Jericho walls we have built. We can ask the Holy Spirit to show us where our unhealthy boundaries lie in our lives, and He will expose them to us.

Nehemiah's task was monumental. The enemy had broken down the walls of Jerusalem and burned the gates with fire. He had to clear rubble, repair walls, build gates, fill in gaps, and completely rebuild some areas. Without any walls or gates, there was no protection from enemies. And it looked as if there was no way to rebuild them—until the king gave Nehemiah all the necessary equipment and supplies to complete the job.

"I also said to the king, 'If it please the king, let me have letters addressed to the governors of the province west of the Euphrates River, instructing them to let me travel safely through their territories on my way to Judah. And please give me a letter addressed to Asaph, the manager of the king's forest, instructing him to give me timber. I will need it to make beams for the gates of the temple fortress, for the city walls, and for a house for myself.' And the king granted these requests because the gracious hand of God was on me" Nehemiah 2:7-8 NLT.

Likewise, our king, Father God, will give us the tools needed to repair our damaged lives. We will explore how rebuilding the wall and gates can help repair our spiritual and emotional health. Remember, Jesus is never overwhelmed by our perceived mess or the amount of work we think is needed to rebuild our lives.

The wall is rebuilt in a specific order—I'm convinced this order was intentional. Following this order, our approach will involve rebuilding the wall and gates one at a time. Each gate will serve as a foundation for the next one. You need the first gate in place to rebuild the wall to the next gate, and so on.

Rebuilding our lives can be challenging, but with the help of the Holy Spirit and our heavenly Father who loves us, we can find the courage and strength to push forward and overcome any obstacles. By gradually rebuilding the walls of our thoughts and emotions, we can begin to see a little beauty in our journey and give thanks to God for guiding us toward recovery.

My greatest hope is that this book might serve as a helpful guide for those looking to deepen their faith and connection with our heavenly Father and find peace in our recovery process.

As you read this book, I humbly ask that you give special consideration to this excerpt from the Holy Scriptures: "And the people of Berea were more open-minded than those in Thessalonica, and they listened eagerly to Paul's message. They searched the Scriptures day after day to see if Paul and Silas were teaching the truth."Acts 17:11 NLT. As we see, the Bereans listened to Paul but then searched the Scriptures themselves to see if the things Paul taught were true. I encourage you to study these Scriptures yourself and ask for God's wisdom in His teachings. I pray our loving heavenly Father will hold you in His arms, heal your broken heart, and bind up your wounds as you seek Him.

"He heals the brokenhearted And binds up their wounds" Psalm 147:3.

## CHAPTER 1
# THE SHEEP GATE

"Then Eliashib the high priest rose up with his brethren the priests and built the Sheep Gate; they consecrated it and hung its doors."
Nehemiah 3:1

The Sheep Gate was the first gate to be restored, and it holds great spiritual significance. It is believed that the name of the gate originated from the fact that it was used as the pathway for the sacrificial lambs in Jewish ceremonies, which were performed for the atonement of sin. This gate foreshadowed Jesus as the Lamb of God who takes away our sins.

"The next day John saw Jesus coming toward him, and said, 'Behold! The Lamb of God who takes away the sin of the world!'" John 1:29.

This gate was consecrated (or set apart as holy) by the high priest, which signifies a special entrance for sacred purposes. The act of setting apart the Sheep Gate by the high priest mirrors Jesus' role as our High Priest, who intercedes for us with God. Through Jesus, believers are set apart and redeemed. He is a mediator between God and people; this enables us to receive Him as our Savior.

So we see that Christ intercedes for us: "Therefore He is also able to save to the uttermost those who come to God through Him, since He always lives to make intercession for them" Hebrews 7:25.

And as the Scriptures affirm, He not only intercedes for us with God, ensuring our salvation, but He is also the compassionate High Priest who understands our weaknesses:

"Inasmuch then as we [believers] have a great High Priest who has [already ascended and] passed through the heavens, Jesus the Son of God, let us hold fast our confession [of faith and cling tenaciously to our absolute trust in Him as Savior]. For we do not have a High Priest who is unable to sympathize and understand our weaknesses and temptations, but One who has been tempted [knowing exactly how it feels to be human] in every respect as we are, yet without [committing any] sin. Therefore let us [with privilege] approach the throne of grace [that is, the throne of God's gracious favor] with confidence and without fear, so that we may receive mercy [for our failures] and find [His amazing] grace to help in time of need [an appropriate blessing, coming just at the right moment]" Hebrews 4:14-16.

Jesus, as High Priest, sets believers apart through redemption. This "setting apart" is beautifully expressed in the book of Hebrews:

"And in accordance with this will [of God] we [who believe in the message of salvation] have been sanctified [that is, set apart as holy for God and His purposes] through the offering of the body of Jesus Christ (the Messiah, the Anointed) once for all" Hebrews 10:10.

The high priest restoring and setting apart the Sheep Gate serves as a powerful illustration of Christ's work in setting believers apart and providing the only pathway to salvation. This visual reminder prompts us to reflect on the boundless love and sacrifice of Jesus, emphasizing that He is the only gate through which we can access eternal life and reconciliation with God. In the Gospel of John, Jesus declares, "I am the gate; whoever enters through me will be saved" John 10:9 NLT.

The Scriptures emphasize that Jesus is the only way to eternal life and reconciliation with God. The Sheep Gate serves as a concrete representation of this vital message, symbolizing the crucial and irreplaceable role of Christ as our High Priest and Savior. As we reflect on the Sheep Gate, let it remind us of the love and sacrifice of Jesus, who is our only pathway to salvation.

Since this gate stands for salvation through Jesus Christ, it is an imperative first step to build this gate in our lives, as it will be the foundation of our faith. We find reconciliation with God through Christ, and it is essential to acknowledge Him as the gateway to our relationship with our Father. Just as sheep depend on a shepherd for protection, guidance, and sustenance, we must rely entirely on Jesus for our spiritual health. Entering through this gate is the first step towards pleasing God and experiencing the abundant life He has for us.

However, even after we accept Christ as Savior and experience salvation, life's hardships and challenges can take a toll on this gate. Our struggles might damage our understanding of God's saving work and cause us to have doubts or feelings of unworthiness. In such moments, it becomes crucial to reflect on the profound sacrifice of Christ on the cross. We need to personalize this gate and understand that Jesus died for each of us individually.

This personal connection is especially significant if you deal with addictions or emotional disorders. If you can recognize that Christ's sacrifice and salvation work is for you, too, it can bring you hope, healing, and restoration. It is essential to thank Him for His saving grace and realize that His sacrifice was for your redemption and freedom from the captivity of sin.

We can strengthen this gate by searching the Scriptures to understand who we are in Christ. In the back of this book, you'll find a few selected passages that tell us who we are in Jesus. The Bible has many passages that reveal our identity and inheritance as children of God. These truths in God's Word remind us that we are deeply loved, completely accepted, and unconditionally forgiven.

We have a covenant with almighty God, and through Christ, we are co-heirs with Him in His kingdom. Embracing these truths helps us stand firm in our faith and empowers us to face life's trials confidently. When we know what Jesus did for us on the cross, we can walk in the freedom and authority He has given us. When we align our thoughts and actions with God's Word, it transforms our lives.

Not only is Jesus our High Priest and the Lamb of God, but He is also our Good Shepherd, as He declared, "I am the good shepherd. The good shepherd sacrifices his life for the sheep" John 10:11 NLT.

Just as sheep follow their shepherd, we must depend entirely on Jesus for our spiritual well-being. Daily reflection on His sacrifice and personalization of the victory that Christ's sacrifice brings to our individual lives will strengthen our understanding of God's love and grace. When we really know our identity in Christ and that we have a covenant with God, it will empower us to live victoriously and walk in the freedom Christ has secured:

"There is therefore now no condemnation to those who are in Christ Jesus, who do not walk according to the flesh, but according to Spirit, for the law of the Spirit of life in Christ Jesus has made me free from the law of sin and death" Romans 8:1-2.

The Sheep Gate and wall represent the spiritual protection and boundaries that guard our hearts and minds. When we accept Jesus as our Savior, it is like repairing and rebuilding a broken or damaged wall. It is the first step toward creating a strong and secure foundation for our faith and relationship with God.

For those who are already Christians, the focus shifts to sustaining and strengthening the wall that God has built through Christ. This maintenance involves actively nurturing our relationship with God through daily practices and intentional efforts.

One way to keep the wall built up and strong is to seek our heavenly Father daily and be mindful of His presence. Prayer, reading His Word, and spending time in worship help us to connect with our Father God on a deeper level. Regularly set aside time to connect with the Father, Son, and Holy Spirit to strengthen your faith and relationship with them.

Including Jesus in all aspects of our lives is another key to maintaining a solid spiritual wall. To include Him means we acknowledge Him as Lord in every decision we make and seek His guidance in both big and small matters. When we involve Jesus in our lives, we show our commitment to follow His ways and align our wills with His.

It is also important to understand that this relationship with God is not based on how we feel or emotions. While emotions will be part of our spiritual walks, the foundation of our relationships with God should be an act of the will, a conscious choice to keep the Father God in our lives. We do this by continually seeking Him, regardless of our emotional states.

We must feed our spirits with God's Word as it is vital for the growth and strength of our spiritual walls. Regularly reading and meditating on biblical scriptures help us gain wisdom, understanding, and discernment. The Word of God becomes the source of nourishment for our souls and will equip us to face challenges and stand firm in our faith.

It's important to remember that building and strengthening our spiritual walls is gradual. Like constructing a wall one stone at a time, our growth in faith and in our relationship with God may not always be instantly obvious. However, each of us can steadily build a healthy and sturdy spiritual wall with consistent effort and a steadfast commitment to seeking God.

So we repair and keep this gate and wall of our spiritual lives by accepting Jesus as our Lord and Savior and actively nurturing our relationships with God. We need to spend time with the Father, Jesus, and the Holy Spirit and involve God in all aspects of our lives to keep our spiritual walls powerful. By feeding our spirits with God's Word and understanding that growth takes time, we can build a firm foundation for our faith and enjoy a deeper relationship with the Father.

"But grow in the grace and knowledge of our Lord and Savior Jesus Christ. To Him be the glory both now and forever. Amen" 2 Peter 3:18.

If you have not accepted Jesus as your Savior, now is a perfect time to do that. "That if you confess with your mouth the Lord Jesus and believe in your heart that God has raised Him from the dead, you will be saved" Romans 10:9.

Admit to God that you are a sinner and want His forgiveness. Believe that Jesus died for your sins. Receive Him as your Lord and Savior, and then thank Him!

Dear heavenly Father,

I come before You humbly, acknowledging that I am a sinner in need of Your forgiveness. I believe that Jesus, Your Son, willingly gave His life on the cross for my sins and that He rose again so that I may receive forgiveness and eternal life through Him.

I wholeheartedly accept Jesus as my Lord and Savior, surrendering my life to His loving guidance and purpose. I invite Him to live in my heart and transform me from the inside out. I am grateful for the gift of salvation and the opportunity to be reconciled with You, Father.

Thank You, Father, for Your grace, mercy, and never-ending love. Please help me to walk in Your ways, honor You with my life, and share the message of Your salvation with others. In Jesus' name, I pray, amen!

If you are a believer but feel like the challenges of life have taken a toll on you spiritually, if the walls and gates of your faith seem battered by the storms of life and circumstances, I encourage you to seek the refuge and strength that can only be found in our Savior, where our Shepherd, Jesus Christ, awaits to restore and renew you.

Bring your brokenness before the Lord and trust in His ability to mend what is shattered. Whether you're facing doubt, heartache, or the weariness of life's blows, this prayer is for you—a prayer for healing, renewal, and a deeper connection with the Father through Christ.

Heavenly Father,

I come before You, seeking the refuge and safety that only You can provide. Thank You for the gift of salvation through Christ, my Shepherd. I acknowledge that as a believer, I, too, face the challenges of life that can batter the walls and gates of my faith.

Lord, strengthen the walls of my faith so that they can stand firm against the storms of doubt, fear, and uncertainty. May the gates of my heart be guarded against the influences that seek to weaken my commitment to You.

Father, I desire a closer relationship with You through Christ. Draw me near to You, that I may experience the fullness of Your love and grace. Reveal any barriers that hinder my communion with You and help me to remove them and walk in the light of Your presence.

Grant me clarity in areas of my life that may be broken and hindering my spiritual growth. Show me the path of righteousness and guide me in the way everlasting. May I be open to Your correction and willing to surrender all that hinders me from fully following You.

I pray for a new beginning spiritually. Renew my heart and mind and lead me into deeper waters of faith. May the Holy Spirit work within me, transforming me into a vessel who glorifies You in all I do. May the walls and gates of my life be a testimony to Your faithfulness and grace.

In the name of Jesus, my precious Good Shepherd, I pray, amen.

## CHAPTER 2

# THE FISH GATE

*"Also, the sons of Hassenaah built the Fish Gate; they laid its beams and hung its doors with its bolts and bars."*

Nehemiah 3:3

After the Sheep Gate, the next gate that was rebuilt was the Fish Gate, where fishermen brought their catches to sell. Salvation is just the beginning; we must strive to become strong soldiers of Jesus Christ and learn to share our faith with others. This involves becoming a fisher of men, reaching out to those around us with the love and truth of the gospel. While not every believer is called to serve as a missionary or church leader, we all have a role to play in bringing others to know God and furthering His kingdom. This is true no matter what your occupation may be.

Whenever an opportunity arises, sharing the gospel with others is essential, even if it makes you uncomfortable. If you feel uneasy about it, begin by praying for your family members, those in leadership positions, missionaries, and those who are lost. Don't worry; sharing your faith will get easier as you grow in the Word and in your relationship with our heavenly Father. As we continue to follow Jesus, He guides us in how to share our faith with others:

And Jesus said to them, "Follow me, and I will make you become fishers of men" Mark 1:17.

The Greek word used in this verse is *ginomai*, and it means to emerge, transition, or become; it suggests a gradual process of training. We begin our growth through discipleship, which means we want to mature and adopt Christlike qualities. Discipleship is a crucial aspect of a believer's journey because it teaches us to live in a way that pleases God and fosters our transformation into Christ's likeness. Through discipleship, we can deepen our faith, gain a deeper understanding of Scripture, and become better equipped to fulfill our calling as followers of Christ.

Your deepening relationship with our heavenly Father is essential and it is what the believer's walk is all about. Sharing your faith, forgiving, and helping others—all these things will be a result of your personal walk with and growth in Christ. Would you like to join me on a spiritual journey and experience growth? We can discover ways to grow and strengthen our relationships with our Father God.

I noticed that the Scripture mentioned that this gate had bolts and bars on it. While locks may have been present on all gates, not all mention using bolts and bars, and this raises the question of why it is noted on some doors while on others, it is not. It is worth examining each gate that mentions bolts and bars a little closer to determine if there may be a reason behind it. For example, locks on the Fish Gate may be a reminder for us to protect our hearts.

The Scripture says, "Guard your heart above all else, for it determines the course of your life" Proverbs 4:23 NLT.

We guard our hearts by abandoning our past selves and keeping God's teachings close. We need to avoid reverting to our former ways of thinking and behaving. We are to bolt and bar our past lives, and put on the new life in Jesus, which will be a day-to-day process; this may not happen overnight. It is a partnership with the Father, Son, and Holy Spirit in our lives each day. If we incorporate the Word into our lives and release things that hold us captive, we can gradually distance ourselves from our old habits and ways.

We also must remain mindful of God's presence throughout the day. God's presence and applying His mighty Word in our lives is the way we lock out the old life. This is important because it's how we move forward in Christ. It is the process of beginning to change our thinking. Changing our thinking will begin to change our actions, and changing our actions can change our lives.

The gates to our souls (our minds and thoughts) are the eyes, ears, and mouth. To continue to grow in Christ, it's crucial to exercise caution concerning the things we allow into our daily lives. We must be aware of what we see, hear, and speak.

## WHAT WE SEE

The eyes are often considered the windows to the soul. First John highlights the sources of worldly influences: "For everything in the world—the lust of the flesh, the lust of the eyes, and the pride of life—comes not from the Father but from the world" 1 John 2:16 NIV.

Being mindful of what you see and watch is important, as it can influence your desires and passions. Therefore, it's best to avoid media, images, and content that encourage unhealthy desires. It's also important to be vigilant against the influences of materialism, arrogance, and the pursuit of worldly success, as they can distract you from your spiritual growth.

## WHAT WE HEAR

The ears play a crucial role in shaping our thoughts and emotions. "So then, my beloved brethren, let every man be swift to hear, slow to speak, slow to wrath" James 1:19.

"Swift to hear" means that we should listen to and follow the teachings of God. This scripture in James emphasizes the importance of actively participating in and paying attention to teachings that align with the principles of God's Word.

Being quick to hear also extends to how we engage with others. It means that we should not only listen to the teachings of the Bible but also listen attentively and lovingly to others, understanding their perspectives, concerns, and experiences. By being swift to hear, we can foster deeper connections with those around us and develop empathy.

Practicing discernment in what we choose to listen to is crucial. We want to filter what we hear. Avoiding gossip, negative talk, and harmful information can help us maintain a spiritual and productive mindset.

We should make an effort to avoid participating in or supporting lies and deception. Listening to falsehoods can misguide our thoughts and lead us astray.

Being aware of what we choose to hear involves avoiding harmful influences and actively seeking godly and constructive input. This approach aligns with the wisdom shared in James 1:19 and contributes to spiritual growth.

## WHAT WE SPEAK

The power of words is emphasized in First Peter 3:10: "He who would love life And see good days, Let him refrain his tongue from evil, And his lips from speaking deceit."

It is important to choose words carefully and avoid any communication that may harm others or your spiritual well-being. Deceitful words can harm relationships and hinder spiritual growth. Speak truthfully, honestly, and in love.

We can cultivate an environment that promotes spiritual growth and aligns with Christian values by being intentional about what we see, hear, and speak. This includes being mindful of the content we allow, the conversations we engage in, and the words we express. Such awareness helps to protect the gates to our souls and enables us to continue growing in Christ.

In addition, we must watch where our feet take us, remembering the places we frequent and the activities we engage in. "Mark out a straight path for your feet; stay on the safe path. Don't get sidetracked; keep your feet from following evil" Proverbs 4:26-27 NLT.

In the same way that our thoughts and emotions can influence our physical actions, the places we go and the activities we engage in can also impact our spiritual journeys. Proverbs 4 advises us to be intentional about the paths we take and avoid any detours that may lead us astray. By staying on the safe path, we can continue to grow in our faith and avoid spiritual pitfalls. Our feet guide us through physical spaces, and it is up to us to make sure we are walking in the right direction toward spiritual growth.

In the book of Nehemiah while they were diligently building the gates, they were also making necessary repairs to strengthen the wall.

"And next to them Meremoth the son of Urijah, the son of Koz, made repairs. Next to them Meshullam the son of Berechiah, the son of Meshezabel, made repairs. Next to them Zadok the son of Baana made repairs" Nehemiah 3:4.

The Hebrew word for repairs in this verse is *chazaq*, it encompasses a powerful concept that goes beyond physical structures like gates and walls. It implies not only restoration but also the act of strengthening, encouraging, and making something strong. Applying this principle can also help us grow spiritually.

In our relationship with our heavenly Father, God desires to strengthen and encourage us through the work of His Holy Spirit within us. Just as the ancient walls and gates of Jerusalem needed repair and reinforcement to withstand external pressures and threats, we, too, encounter various challenges and trials in our lives. We might face circumstances that test our faith and leave us feeling broken or damaged.

Throughout our lifetimes, we may have experienced hurt and pain caused by others, leaving emotional scars that need healing. God wants to be our ultimate source of healing and restoration by His boundless love and mercy. When we come to Him, admitting our brokenness and seeking His forgiveness and grace, He begins the process of rebuilding us.

This verse in Ephesians reminds us of the purpose of the church: " ... for the equipping of the saints, for the work of ministry, for the edifying of the body of Christ" Ephesians 4:12.

This "equipping" goes beyond just teaching; it involves preparation, strengthening, and making something usable. God wants to mold us into strong vessels, empowered by His Spirit and ready to be useful in His kingdom. As we embrace God's repairing work in our lives, we find that our weaknesses and past hurts become opportunities for growth and change. Through His loving guidance, we find strength, and our faith is made solid.

We become equipped to face life's challenges with resilience, knowing that God's strength and grace sustain us. In this process of repair and equipping, we must learn to extend forgiveness and love to others, just as we have received it from our heavenly Father. We become channels of His healing and restoration to those around us and instruments of reconciliation and hope in a broken world.

So let us humbly come before our loving heavenly Father, acknowledging our need for repair and inviting Him to strengthen, encourage, and rebuild us. May we be vessels ready to be used by Him for His purposes, bringing glory to His name and spreading His love and grace to all we meet.

Here is another fascinating and important verse: "Next to them the Tekoites made repairs; but their nobles did not put their shoulders to the work of their Lord". Nehemiah 3:5

Tekoa was an ancient town located in the tribe of Judah and nestled on the range of hills near Hebron. It stretched eastward toward the Dead Sea and was a familiar community to the Israelites of Nehemiah's time, as mentioned in 2 Chronicles 11:6.

In Tekoa, there was a noticeable difference between the ordinary people and the nobles. While the everyday citizens toiled tirelessly, laboring with their hands and hearts to contribute to building the walls, the nobles, in their privileged positions, stubbornly refused to partake in these endeavors. They disregarded their responsibilities, showing a lack of concern for their fellow citizens and an unwillingness to align their actions with God's will.

This example serves as a wise analogy for our own lives today. Just like those nobles, we face choices daily—whether to embrace our roles and responsibilities or to shy away from the effort needed to fulfill them. In our pursuit of wholeness through Jesus, we are faced with a powerful truth: The path to spiritual growth and fulfillment demands effort and dedication.

Wholeness is what God meant us to have from the beginning, but sin entered the world and fragmented our souls. But we have the blessed hope that by embracing the teachings of Jesus and allowing the Holy Spirit to nurture the fruits of love, compassion, and forgiveness in us, we can begin our restoration. But this will require intentional effort by us.

Achieving spiritual growth and wholeness requires a personal journey. It requires reflection, prayer, and perseverance. We must confront our weaknesses, acknowledge our flaws, and take steps toward self-discipline. No one else can walk this path for us; we are responsible for our actions.

Following Jesus goes beyond mere lip service or occasional good deeds. It calls for a deep commitment to living out His teachings in every aspect of our lives. Just as the ordinary people in Tekoa worked diligently to manifest their faith through action, we must do the same. Our faith in Jesus should be evident in how we treat others, our willingness to serve, and our walking in love.

Achieving wholeness and following Jesus requires active engagement and personal investment. We must not be like the nobles who shunned their responsibilities, but rather embrace the opportunity to contribute, grow, and embody the principles of love, compassion, and humility. By doing so, we can find true fulfillment in our lives and become beacons of light and inspiration to others.

In stark contrast to the nobles, Baruch the son of Zabbai, wholeheartedly undertook the task of restoration. He demonstrated fervent dedication as he diligently made repairs.

"Next to him was Baruch son of Zabbai, who zealously repaired an additional section from the angle to the door of the house of Eliashib the high priest" Nehemiah 3:20 NLT.

The word *zealously* used here means to burn, blaze up. It is to work with passion. With determination, Baruch dedicated himself to the task of repairing the wall. He approached his work daily with a burning zeal that ignited his spirit and fueled his efforts. He recognized the immense significance of the outcome and its impact on the community, motivating him to take the responsibility seriously.

I like to think he would arrive each day fully aware of the weight of his duty. With a clear vision in mind and a committed heart, he immersed himself in building the wall, laboring tirelessly with unwavering focus. The wall was not just a structure to him; it symbolized unity, protection, and a strong, immovable foundation. His determination remained steadfast. The challenges that arose along the way were nothing more than stepping stones for him to overcome, and he embraced them. He was willing to do whatever it took to complete the restoration.

So we see that some of the nobles were not interested in reconstructing the wall and chose to delegate that task to others. However, we see Baruch's unwavering dedication to the project. His commitment is a powerful reminder of the impact an individual can have.

We can all take a lesson from Baruch's passion and dedication. Let us welcome rebuilding our walls enthusiastically, knowing that the smallest tasks, when approached with zeal, can lead to the most remarkable achievements. Let's be like Baruch and not the nobles. Let's kindle fires of determination within ourselves and build our walls stone by stone.

As Christians, surrendering ourselves to God in every aspect of our lives can be difficult. Nonetheless, it is what we strive for even when faced with hardship; we must choose to follow Christ. Our goal should be to have a heavenly outlook instead of an earthly one in every situation.

Having a heavenly perspective involves seeing the world and our lives through God's eternal view. It means aligning our thoughts, actions, and desires with the values and principles of God's kingdom. By doing so, we prioritize eternal significance over temporary pleasures, seeking spiritual growth and God's will in all aspects of our lives. This heavenly or kingdom perspective, rooted in biblical truths, guides us in making choices that contribute to the flourishing of our souls and the progression of God's kingdom on earth.

Each time we surrender to God's authority, we continue to learn and grow in His teachings through the Holy Spirit. This ongoing process only stops once we are in heaven with the Lord. Remember that God is a loving Father, who always has our best interests at heart. We want to pursue and cultivate a deep and meaningful relationship with our heavenly Father: "But seek first the kingdom of God and his righteousness, and all these things will be added to you" Matthew 6:33.

"Search for the Lord and for his strength; continually seek him" 1 Chronicles 16:11 NLT.

Let's put our shoulders to the work and seek His kingdom first; the fruit of the Spirit will flow from our relationship with our heavenly Father; this is the key. Let's continually seek Him and always remember that nothing can separate us from Him.

"And I am convinced that nothing can ever separate us from

God's love. Neither death nor life, neither angels nor demons, neither our fears for today nor our worries about tomorrow—not even the powers of hell can separate us from God's love. No power in the sky above or in the earth below—indeed, nothing in all creation will ever be able to separate us from the love of God that is revealed in Christ Jesus our Lord" Romans 8:38-39 NLT.

As we reflect on the unbreakable bond of God's love, let us carry this assurance into our daily lives, knowing that nothing can separate us from Him. May our actions and choices always be guided by the wonderful love revealed in Christ Jesus our Lord.

Dear heavenly Father,

I am grateful for the journey so far. I pray for boldness to share the gospel fearlessly and to be a light in the darkness around me. Strengthen my faith, Lord; deepen it in the waters of Your grace.

Teach me to guard my heart, Father. Help me be discerning in what I allow into my life, keeping it pure and focused on You. May my words be a reflection of Your love, and where I've faltered, grant me the humility to repent and seek restoration.

Give me the willingness to do what it takes to grow spiritually and to invest time in Your Word, prayer, and fellowship with You. Open my eyes to see things from Your perspective, aligning my will with Yours.

In Jesus' name, I pray, amen.

# CHAPTER 3
# THE OLD GATE

> *"Moreover, Jehoiada the son of Paseah and Meshullam the son of Besodeiah repaired the Old Gate; they laid its beams and hung its doors, with its bolts and bars."*
> Nehemiah 3:6

The only place in the Bible where it is called the Old Gate is in Nehemiah. The purpose it served is unknown. I think it is a perfect symbol of the old man in our lives. I believe even the gate's name, "Old Gate," symbolizes the presence of the "old man," which refers to our former selves, characterized by worldly desires, sinful habits, and ungodly attitudes. In our pursuit of spiritual growth, we must undergo a transformation, which the Bible calls the renewal of our minds. We can only achieve this change by aligning with God's Word and obediently walking in His teachings.

Again, we see bolts and bars mentioned on the Old Gate, perhaps to remind us that we are called to lock out the influences of the old man. To do this, we can take steps like these:

Intentionally distance ourselves from ungodly influences.

Break free from unhealthy patterns.

Resist temptations that once defined our lives.

Through God's grace and the power of His Word and His

Son, we can overcome these challenges and embrace a new way of thinking.

To build on the foundation laid by the Fish Gate, where we learn to read and apply God's Word and share our faith with others, the Old Gate takes us to the next level of spiritual growth. At this stage, we focus on developing a deeper understanding of God's Word and applying it to our daily lives.

By immersing ourselves in Scripture, studying its principles, and committing verses to memory, we equip ourselves to align with God's will. As we delve deeper into the Word, we discover the truth about our new identity in Christ. The Scriptures reveal how wonderful our new creation is, the blessings of salvation, and the abundant life God has called us to live. Armed with this knowledge, we learn how to live in a manner that reflects our new nature in Christ.

Yet the process of growth continues beyond merely gaining knowledge. The Old Gate also reminds us to seek God's guidance in recognizing areas in our lives that require change. Through prayer and searching our hearts, we open ourselves to God's life-changing work in us. We invite Him to reveal areas where we need to throw off old behaviors, attitudes, and mindsets that do not align with His perfect plan for us.

The Old Gate serves as a reminder that it represents the need to let go of the old man and embrace the new creation in Christ. Through diligent study of God's Word and submission to His guidance, we allow Him to work within us, molding us into His likeness daily. As we progress through this gate, our goal is to become living testimonies of God's grace, reflecting His light and love to the world around us. Let's explore what Scripture says about this transformation:

"And do not be conformed to this world, but be transformed by the renewing of your mind, that you may prove what is that good and acceptable and perfect will of God" Romans 12:2.

## BUT BE TRANSFORMED

To be transformed means to adopt new habits and behaviors guided by the power of the Holy Spirit rather than falling back into old ways. This requires a radical shift in how we think. As we reflect on this process of renewal, the comparison of old and new wineskins becomes a powerful illustration of the changes that God desires in our lives.

"And no one puts new wine into old wineskins. For the old skins would burst from the pressure, spilling the wine and ruining the skins. New wine is stored in new wineskins so that both are preserved" Matthew 9:17 NLT.

We often run into obstacles that delay our spiritual growth and block our connection with our heavenly Father. These can hinder us and be compared to old wineskins — constricting, rigid, and unable to accommodate the new and life-changing experiences the Lord wishes to pour into our lives. Let's dig a little deeper into each aspect:

**Old Ways of Thinking:** Throughout life, we develop specific mental patterns and belief systems influenced by our upbringing, culture, and experiences. These firmly established thought processes sometimes limit our understanding of God's truth and stunt our spiritual progress. We must be willing to challenge and replace these outdated thought patterns with a deeper understanding of

God's principles.

**Religious ideas not based on Scripture:** While some religious traditions and teachings can be helpful, they can also include interpretations or practices that deviate from the core teachings of Scripture. Transformation is a path that involves the Holy Spirit giving us discernment so we can evaluate our religious beliefs, ensuring they align with the true message of the Word of God.

**Bad habits:** Over time, we can develop habits detrimental to our well-being and spiritual growth. These habits can include unhealthy thought patterns, addictive behaviors, or self-destructive tendencies. Transformation requires us to acknowledge and replace these negative patterns with life-giving habits that nurture our relationship with God and others.

**Emotional baggage:** Past hurts, unresolved trauma, and emotional wounds can act as heavy burdens that weigh us down and prevent us from moving forward in our spiritual growth. Letting go of emotional baggage and seeking healing and restoration is crucial to creating a new wineskin within ourselves. As we invite God's love and grace into our hearts, He helps us release the emotional burdens, allowing us to experience genuine transformation.

**New wineskin:** Just as new wine requires a new wineskin to expand and mature properly, our spiritual growth demands a pliable and receptive heart. As we embrace change and transformation, we create room for God's Spirit to work within us, molding us into vessels capable of receiving and radiating His love, wisdom, and grace.

**Being pliable and stretched by the Lord:** Being stretched involves surrendering ourselves to God's guidance, allowing Him to stretch and mold us according to His divine plan. Sometimes this process can be uncomfortable, requiring us to step outside our comfort zones and face challenges that refine our character and deepen our faith. If we are able to embrace this stretching, it will enable us to grow in ways we never thought possible and become vessels fit for God's purposes.

If we can recognize and release old wineskins, our outdated thinking, religious ideas, bad habits, and emotional baggage, we create space for God to bring about rebuilding within us. This pliability and openness to His leading enable us to grow and mature in our faith, becoming vessels that can hold and pour out the abundant blessings He wants to bestow upon us.

By renewing your mind, you embark on a journey that will transform your thoughts, causing personal and spiritual growth. It calls for a fundamental shift in our thought processes, beliefs, and attitudes, leading to a more godly way of living. We must first recognize the need to change our current mindset to achieve this renewal. Our past experiences and ingrained habits shape many of our thoughts and actions. These patterns may not always align with God's Word and principles. We need to identify areas that require reconstruction.

Taking on a new perspective involves breaking free from the shackles of negative thoughts, self-limiting beliefs, and impulsive behavior. Rather than being driven solely by emotions or feelings, we should strive to make decisions rooted in faith and trust in God. Faith encourages us to relinquish control and surrender to God, where we can find peace in times of uncertainty and strength during challenges.

This renewing of the mind is not a one-time event but an ongoing process that demands consistent effort. Each day presents new opportunities to align our thoughts and actions with God's Word. It requires a commitment to being mindful of our thoughts, words, and deeds, examining them in the light of God's Word.

The walk of faith-filled decision-making may seem daunting, especially when we're faced with trials or temptations. Yet even when we stumble and fall short of our ideals, we can continue to progress. The path toward renewal is not about perfection but about a genuine desire to grow spiritually. Each step we take, however small, brings us closer to a deeper understanding of our purpose and a closer connection to our loving heavenly Father.

Central to this process is the role of the Holy Spirit. He will provide us with strength, wisdom, and comfort during the times we struggle. His ever-present divine help instills confidence in us that we are not alone in this renewal process. As we begin this new journey, we have an invaluable resource in the Word to guide us. The Word instructs us to renew our minds, showing that we are capable of doing so. This call to renew our minds opens the door for us to experience a deeper understanding of the Scriptures and a more meaningful walk with the Lord.

Through renewing our minds by reading the Word, making faith-based choices, and relying on the support of the Holy Spirit, we enter a path of spiritual growth. The process may be challenging and require consistent effort, but each step we take brings us closer to the goal of a deeper relationship with the Father, Jesus, and the Holy Spirit. This is the narrow path Jesus warned us about.

"Enter by the narrow gate; for wide is the gate and broad is the way that leads to destruction, and there are many who go in by it. Because narrow is the gate and difficult is the way which leads to life, and there are few who find it" Matthew 7:13-14.

Let's welcome the experiences and lessons we can learn on this path with humility, gratitude, and an unwavering commitment to renewing our minds.

"... that you put off, concerning your former conduct, the old man which grows corrupt according to the deceitful lusts, and be renewed in the spirit of your mind, and that you put on the new man which was created according to God, in true righteousness and holiness" Ephesians 4:22-24.

We have the Holy Spirit to guide and empower us to become that new man. But it takes work and faith choices to grow. You may have a lot of baggage, and you may even feel sometimes, like me, that you're an emotional wreck, but we still have the choice of choosing God's way or our way.

Consider this scripture that also guides us on the path of the new man: "Then Jesus said to His disciples, 'If anyone desires to come after Me, let him deny himself, and take up his cross, and follow Me' " Matthew 16:24.

## LET HIM DENY HIMSELF

Another aspect of the renewing process is denying yourself. Have you ever wondered what it means to deny yourself? Denying yourself is a process that requires a certain level of self-discipline and self-denial. It involves letting go of old habits and behaviors that hold us back and embracing new ways of thinking and acting. This can be a challenge, but it is necessary if we want to grow spiritually. By practicing self-denial, we learn to prioritize God over our goals, desires, and impulses. Denying ourselves will help us develop greater willpower, focus, resilience, and reliance on

Jesus, and it is a key part of the journey.

I strive to prioritize God in my life by dedicating time to daily devotion, especially through prayer. This commitment, while seemingly simple, is a significant challenge. My mind often becomes preoccupied with various tasks, making it difficult to maintain focus on God. My thoughts frequently wander, and I find myself constantly redirecting my mind. This struggle, which perhaps some of you can relate to, is an example of denying oneself - setting aside time for prayer requires self-discipline and the willingness to let go of distractions and worldly concerns. Despite the challenges, I persist in this practice because I understand its significance in fortifying my faith and preparing me to withstand tests of belief.

The ultimate goal of prioritizing daily devotion and practicing self-discipline is to stand firm in our faith, even amidst adversity. This discipline is essential for strengthening our faith and making us ready to face trials with conviction.

It might seem like a daunting task, but the truth is that emotional healing and growth require effort. Similarly, building a relationship with our heavenly Father also takes work. It might help to think of yourself like this: *I am a spirit, I have a soul, I live in a body.* Once you accept Jesus as Savior, your spirit is saved, the soul (the mind, your ways of thinking) must be renewed by the Word, and the body will one day be redeemed.

Denying yourself does not mean you must stuff your emotions, feelings, and thoughts. We want to take them to God and confess them to Him first. He knows what you think and feel anyway, so be honest with Him. Acknowledge your feelings, then make a faith choice to follow Jesus. It means you choose to lay down whatever is getting in the way of your walk with Christ. It may be fear, anxiety, doubt, anger, addiction, or unforgiveness. Ask the Holy Spirit to show you your stumbling blocks and how they prevent you from moving forward. Ask Him to give you a kingdom perspective (seeing things from God's point of view).

## TAKE UP HIS CROSS

The meaning of taking up one's cross is significant. In Jesus' time, a cross symbolized suffering, shame, and death. Jesus exemplified this by willingly carrying the heavy burden of the cross on which He would be crucified. This act of self-sacrifice demonstrates that He would never ask us to do anything He hadn't already done Himself. When He instructs His disciples to "take up their cross," He tells them to be willing to endure hardship for the sake of following Him.

Jesus instructs us to "pick up our cross" as a powerful symbol of obedience to the Father and submission to His divine will. It symbolizes a complete commitment to the cause of Christ, even if it means personal sacrifice and discomfort. Therefore, when we take up our crosses, we follow in our Lord's footsteps, embracing a life of obedience and surrender to God's plan, just as Jesus did. It involves an active and intentional commitment to live following His teachings, example, and mission. It means aligning one's life with the values, principles, and mission of Jesus Christ.

Taking up your cross to follow Jesus is about submission to His Word and will, but it goes beyond mere submission. It's a call to radical discipleship, where a person's allegiance to Christ takes precedence over everything else.

Taking up the cross involves surrendering control of one's life to God. It means acknowledging that God's plans and purposes are greater and more significant than ours. It is a willingness to endure difficulties and even persecution for the gospel's sake and the advancement of God's kingdom. Following Jesus involves:

> A lifelong walk of growing in faith
> Learning from Him
> Imitating His character
> Actively taking part in His mission

Taking up the cross expresses genuine discipleship and devotion to Jesus. It's a call to live a life that reflects His love, grace, and truth in a world that often opposes these values. It's a reminder that following Jesus may involve challenges and hardships, but the rewards of eternal life and a deeper relationship with God far outweigh any temporary difficulties. I think my husband is a good example of living out this principle.

There was a time when my husband faced ridicule for his faith, encountering some particularly hurtful comments. One of the frequent comments he endured was, 'Only a fool would believe in an all-powerful deity.' Despite the pressure to conform or even pretend to agree with the ridicule, he chose a different path. Instead of caving in, he seized the opportunity to stand firm in his beliefs and refused to deny or compromise his faith in Jesus.

## AND FOLLOW ME

Choosing to follow Jesus is not just a one-time decision but an adventure that unfolds each day with a renewed commitment to move forward in His love and grace. It's acknowledging that our pasts, no matter how checkered or imperfect, don't define us, for Jesus offers the promise of forgiveness and redemption, allowing us to break free from the chains of guilt and regret. By choosing to follow and surrender to Jesus, we learn to let go of the burdens that weigh us down.

By making this choice daily, we develop a deeper understanding of God's love and His purpose for our lives, knowing that God's love is unconditional and covers all our shortcomings. Along the way, we discover incredible power in the grace of His love, which not only heals our wounds but also enables us to extend that same love and grace to others. I think these verses in Philippians say it so well in the New Living Translation:

"Dear friends, you always followed my instructions when I was with you. And now that I am away, it is even more important. Work hard to show the results of your salvation, obeying God with deep reverence and fear. For God is working in you, giving you the desire and the power to do what pleases him" Philippians 2:12-13 NLT.

"And I am certain that God, who began the good work within you, will continue his work until it is finally finished on the day when Christ Jesus returns" Philippians 1:6 NLT.

In these scriptures, Paul beautifully captures the essence of the Christian walk. It is easy to feel isolated and alone in life, especially when facing challenges or uncertainties. However, for us who believe in Christ, there is assurance that we are never truly alone. The presence of God in our lives brings comfort, strength, and hope.

God has started a good work within you and will carry it through if you give the Holy Spirit your permission and cooperation. This process starts when we accept Christ as our Savior and continues as we grow spiritually. While God's grace starts this work, your willingness to work with Him is crucial for its success.

Through the power of the Holy Spirit, God starts a beautiful process of renewing our hearts, minds, and spirits. He begins to shape us into the image of Christ, reshaping our character and molding us into vessels of His love and grace. This process can involve challenges, trials, and even moments of uncertainty, but God is faithful and will never abandon us.

Our cooperation is vital; God doesn't force transformation on us. Instead, He invites us into a loving and intimate partnership. When we willingly surrender to His leading and align our hearts with His will, we open the door for Him to transform us and work more powerfully in our lives.

He reassures us that His presence goes with us every step of the way. In times of joy, He rejoices with us, and in times of sorrow, He comforts us. We are never alone in facing life's challenges. God walks beside us, guiding and supporting us through the ups and downs.

How does God comfort or guide us? His support can manifest in various ways, such as through timely words from friends or through personal experiences with scripture. Recently, I was grappling with multiple emotional struggles and feeling overwhelmed. In a moment of desperation, I questioned if God was truly attentive to my pain and concerns. In the middle of my uncertainty, I turned to prayer and sought reassurance. The answer came to me through Psalm 116:2 NLT: "Because he bends down to listen, I will pray as long as I have breath." This revelation brought me comfort and renewed strength, affirming that God was indeed present and caring and was there, especially in my trials.

In moments of doubt or when we feel overwhelmed, it is essential to remember that God's love and grace are steadfast.

His promise to never leave nor forsake us is a source of great comfort and strength. As we rely on His presence and lean on His understanding, we find the courage to press on, knowing that he will reward our faithfulness.

I love this next verse, and it becomes especially meaningful in our quest to change: "Next to them Jedaiah the son of Harumaph made repairs in front of his house. And next to him Hattush the son of Hashabniah made repairs" Nehemiah 3:10 NKJV.

This passage beautifully highlights the importance of repairing what is in front of us, as emphasized more than once in chapter 3 of Nehemiah. It reminds us that our spiritual growth begins right where we are, at "our" house. Our only responsibility is to say "yes" and allow the work to begin. God has abundant time and patience to guide us as we mature at our own pace.

In Christ, we are never alone. God has begun a good work within us, and as we cooperate with Him, He continues to shape us into vessels of His love and grace. With each step we take, God's presence stays a consistent source of comfort, guidance, and assurance, leading us toward the day we will be united with Him for eternity.

Dear heavenly Father,

I seek Your guidance and strength for the changes I need to make in my life. Grant me the courage to walk in the new man, leaving behind the burdens of the old. Help me to break the unhealthy patterns in my life and turn away from temptation.

Lord, I desire transformation through the renewing of my mind in Your Word. May Your truth be my compass, guiding my thoughts and actions. I surrender to Your will and choose to take up my cross, even when the path seems difficult. Help me truly choose to follow Christ, committing myself wholeheartedly to this journey of faith.

In Jesus' name, I pray, amen.

# CHAPTER 4
# THE VALLEY GATE

*"Hanun and the inhabitants of Zanoah repaired the Valley Gate.
They built it, hung its doors with its bolts and bars,
And repaired a thousand cubits of the wall as far as the Refuse Gate."
Nehemiah 3:13*

To be better prepared for the challenges that lie ahead, we must first pass through the three preceding gates. These gates serve as the building blocks of our spiritual journeys, paving the way toward the valley gate. They also signify a milestone in our spiritual walk, indicating growth, trust in the Lord, and the beginning of placing our faith in Him.

Some believe that this gate was connected to the Hinnom and Kidron Valleys, which historically held a dark and ominous significance. Kidron means murky, dusky, and gloomy. Many people once used the valley for idol worship rituals that involved sacrificing children through burning. It was also where they disposed of animal remains. It stood for a place of despair, hopelessness, and moral degradation.

Symbolically, this valley gate represents the trials and tough times we encounter in life. It reminds us that we will face challenges, struggles, and moments of darkness that might test our faith. However, the message is clear—we must remain steadfast in our trust and belief in our powerful God during these trying times. Rather than succumbing to despair, it is an opportunity to fortify our faith and deepen our connection with Him.

When we travel through this symbolic valley, the Scriptures urge us to discard any idols we might have constructed in our lives. These idols represent anything that takes precedence over God in our hearts, whether material possessions, personal ambitions, or other worldly attachments.

"Therefore put to death your members which are on the earth: fornication, uncleanness, passion, evil desire, and covetousness, which is idolatry" Colossians 3:5.

By eliminating these distractions and destructive influences, we create space for God to work in us, strengthening our relationships with Him and enabling us to face life's challenges with grace and courage.

Maintaining a kingdom perspective in the valleys entails viewing our circumstances through the eyes of faith and understanding that God's plans are greater than our own. While the valleys may be daunting, Scripture reminds us to keep our eyes fixed on Jesus. By doing so, we recognize that He is our guide, comforter, and source of strength. He walks alongside us in our darkest moments. With Jesus as our support, we can overcome the trials we encounter on our lives' journeys, emerging stronger, wiser, and more spiritually mature.

The Valley Gate serves as a great spiritual lesson. It teaches us to rely on God's guidance and grace, recognizing that every challenge we face is an opportunity for growth and transformation. As we remain faithful to our heavenly Father and keep our hearts tuned to Him, we can confidently face the challenges of life with courage, hope, and the assurance that God will be with us every step of the way. This will help us develop a deeper and more fulfilling relationship with Him.

Upon returning to Jerusalem, Nehemiah inspected the damage to the wall by going out at night through the Valley Gate.

"And I went out by night through the Valley Gate to the Serpent Well and the Refuse Gate and viewed the walls of Jerusalem which were broken down and its gates which were burned with fire" Nehemiah 2:13.

In this valley, he saw the destruction and rubble that lay before him, blocking his path to restoration. This imagery can be likened to any adversity or overwhelming circumstances we meet.

The mention of "bolts and bars" on this door suggests the need to protect ourselves from negative influences and emotions, like doubt, fear, and defeat. We must lock out these destructive elements from our minds and hearts to overcome these challenges and achieve restoration or growth.

Most of us are familiar with this scripture from Isaiah: "But those who wait on the Lord shall renew their strength; They shall mount up with wings like eagles, They shall run and not be weary, They shall walk and not faint" Isaiah 40:31.

This verse emphasizes the power of faith and patience in waiting on the Lord. It leads to the renewal of strength and the ability to persevere through difficult times, providing hope and encouragement. However, let us look at the verse that precedes Isaiah 40:31: "He gives power to the weak, and to those who have no might, He increases strength" Isaiah 40:29.

This verse reminds us that even when we feel weak or lacking in strength, we can find solace and empowerment through our relationship with God. The broader message conveyed here is that seeking guidance and support from our heavenly Father can be a source of strength and comfort in times of hardship and challenges. Paul's teachings in Philippians 4:11-13 further reinforce the idea that through Christ, we can find contentment and strength in all situations. This means we can draw upon our faith as we face life's trials, trusting that our heavenly Father will never abandon us.

Nehemiah's passage through the Valley Gate to inspect severely broken wall and burned gates emphasizes how important it is to recognize and confront any obstacles that impede our paths to restoration. By keeping doubt, fear, and defeat at bay and instead relying on our faith in God, we can draw strength and contentment to overcome any challenges we may face. The apostle Paul beautifully echoed this sentiment, reminding us that we, too, can learn the secret of contentment in every situation through the strength we receive from Christ:

"Not that I was ever in need, for I have learned how to be content with whatever I have. I know how to live on almost nothing or with everything. I have learned the secret of living in every situation, whether it is with a full stomach or empty, with plenty or little, for I can do everything through Christ, who gives me strength" Philippians 4:11-13 NLT.

Not only are we encouraged to be content, but this Scripture in the book of James also tells us to count it all joy when facing trials. "My brethren, count it all joy when you fall into various trials, knowing that the testing of your faith produces patience" James 1:2-3.

Really? Count it all joy? In a place brimming with misery and discouragement, why are we encouraged to have joy? How are we supposed to be happy when we are in a valley full of trials? At first glance, this notion of finding joy in difficult circumstances can be perplexing and even confusing. After all, how can one be joyful during trials, hardships, or times filled with hopelessness?

"Count it all joy" is a term that means to evaluate, to consider. When James encourages believers to "count it all joy," he invites us to evaluate our response to trials and consider the deeper purpose behind our struggles. The idea is to view trials as opportunities for growth and spiritual development. To fully grasp this concept, embracing the perspective of having faith and trust in God is essential. Instead of allowing difficulties to crush our spirits, James encourages us to turn to God, trusting in His strength and wisdom to guide us through challenging times.

It's essential to differentiate between worldly joy and the joy that the Holy Spirit provides. Worldly joy often depends on external circumstances and is fleeting. In contrast, joy from the Holy Spirit is rooted in the knowledge that God is in control and He is working things out for our good, even during trials. This spiritual joy assures us that we are not alone in our struggles and that God is present, listening, and caring for us.

It's not about pretending to be happy amid pain or suffering but rather about choosing how we respond to those challenges and difficulties. Feeling overwhelmed, sad, or anxious is normal in times of trial. "Count it all joy" doesn't mean suppressing these emotions or putting on a facade that everything is fine. Instead, it's an invitation to approach our challenges with a mindset of faith, hope, and trust in God's promises. It's recognizing that God can use even difficult circumstances to shape and refine our character, leading us to a deeper relationship with Him and greater spiritual maturity.

So "Count it all joy" is about finding hope amid adversity and embracing the truth that God is with us through every valley we encounter. By focusing on Jesus and His promises, we can go through trials with strength, knowing that He will never abandon us and is continually at work in our lives, leading us toward a deeper understanding of His love and grace.

This scripture in James encourages us to consider how we will choose to respond to the trouble we face, to look at our situation from a different perspective, and to adjust our attitudes. Are we keeping our eyes on Jesus, trusting Him to bring us through? Are we trusting in His Word that He is going to strengthen us?

This joy is the knowledge that the Father is in control and hears us no matter what. He knows the valley we are in, and He isn't going to leave us there. We will have troubles and trials because the Word says we will. But we can go through them with hope and in His strength.

Expressing gratitude towards God is easy when everything is going great, but what about when we face tough times? Have you ever taken a moment to thank God for the trials or challenges you were facing? I must admit that I'm not always the most cheerful and grateful person during difficult times. However, I am committed to practicing gratitude and offering praise to God even when things aren't going as planned. I trust that my faithful heavenly Father understands my struggles and is working through them for my personal growth.

The Word of God offers abundant guidance on dealing with trials. Here are a few examples:

"And not only that, we also glory in tribulations, knowing that tribulation produces perseverance, and perseverance character; and character, hope. Now hope does not disappoint, because the love of God has been poured out in our hearts by the Holy Spirit who was given to us." Romans 5:3-4

"He comforts us in all our troubles so that we can comfort others. When they are troubled, we will be able to give them the same comfort God has given us." 2 Corinthians 1:4

"Beloved, do not think it strange concerning the fiery trial which is to try you, as though some strange thing happened to you; but rejoice to the extent that you partake of Christ's sufferings, that when His glory is revealed, you may also be glad with exceeding joy." 1 Peter 4:12-13

"... strengthening the souls of the disciples, exhorting them to continue in the faith, and saying, 'We must through many tribulations enter the kingdom of God." Acts 14:22

"He will not be afraid of evil tidings: his heart is steadfast trusting in the Lord." Psalm 112:7

This verse in Psalms that I often relate to describes the overwhelming feelings of despair, a deep yearning, and a sense of hopelessness. It speaks to searching for answers and grappling with the unknown and has always resonated with me.

"Deep calls unto deep at the noise of Your waterfalls; All Your waves and billows have gone over me." Psalm 42:7

In times of great distress, my first response used to be a desire for it to go away and stop. However, I have come to a new understanding. What if, instead of asking for relief from God, my emotional turmoil is a call to delve deeper into my faith and seek a greater understanding of God's teachings? Rather than seeking shallow waters, perhaps I should embrace the tumultuous depths where I feel far from God and answers seem elusive. Is it possible that my healing may require personal transformation and a willingness to remain steadfast in my faith, even during adversity? My answer is yes; I believe it will.

Finally, if we little by little learn to trust in our heavenly Father during our most challenging times and remember that we are never alone and He only has our best interest in mind, we will grow and become stronger spiritually and emotionally. In times of difficulty, we can gradually build our trust in our heavenly Father. With faith, determination, and the Holy Spirit's help, we can overcome any problem and emerge stronger, and we will learn to navigate through these challenging times a little more easily.

This scripture reminds us that we are blessed and greatly favored when we draw strength from God and keep our hearts fixed on Him. By focusing on the temporary nature of life and fixing our gaze on Jesus, who can guide us through any obstacle, we discover that even in the midst of hardships, God transforms our struggles into opportunities for blessings and renewal,

> "Blessed and greatly favored is the man whose strength is in You,
> In whose heart are the highways to Zion.
> Passing through the Valley of Weeping [Baca], they make it a place of springs;
> The early rain also covers it with blessings.
> They go from strength to strength [increasing in victorious power];
> Each of them appears before God in Zion." Psalm 84:5-7 AMP
> Dear Heavenly Father,

I turn to You for strength and guidance during any trial that may come my way. Help me see these difficulties as opportunities to grow, not to fear, but to "count it all joy" by considering my response in faith, not doubt.

In moments of trial, even though I may express my emotions and cry out, grant me the courage to face the challenge and, above all, instill in me the assurance that I am not alone. May I determine to keep my focus on You, my heavenly Father, trusting that Your wisdom and love accompany me through every valley.

In Jesus' name, I pray, amen.

# CHAPTER 5
# THE REFUSE GATE

*"Malchijah the son of Rechab, leader of the district of Beth Haccerem, repaired the Refuse Gate; he built it and hung its doors with its bolts and bars."*

Nehemiah 3:14

The Refuse or Dung Gate led out of the city down to the valley of Hinnom (the same dismal location we encountered at the Valley Gate). This gate serves as a great example of getting rid of garbage. Often, trash was burned, making it impossible to reuse.

During our time at the Valley Gate, we began to learn to identify and conquer uncertainty and skepticism by having faith in God in moments of adversity. At the Refuse Gate, we take the things that hinder our walk and surrender them to the Father. We also must get rid of whatever garbage may be blocking us spiritually, or it might destroy us.

As Christians, it's important that we only allow things that align with God's Word to be a part of our lives. Anything that hinders our spiritual growth should be considered useless and discarded as garbage. The gate also mentions the need for bolts and bars, which represent the need to secure our lives against this garbage. By locking and bolting out the junk, we can rid ourselves of the trash. Just like how trash is burned or removed so it can never be used again, we need to let go of things that hold us back and ensure they don't find their way back inside.

What things in our lives block out the Holy Spirit working in us? What does God's Word say about the garbage we may have in life that we must dispose of through the refuse gate? The garbage may include what we watch or talk about and the thoughts we dwell on.

Let's examine a few scriptures that illustrate what junk in our lives might appear like.

"Let all bitterness and wrath and anger and clamor [perpetual animosity, resentment, strife, fault-finding] and slander be put away from you, along with every kind of malice [all spitefulness, verbal abuse, malevolence]. Be kind and helpful to one another, tender-hearted [compassionate, understanding], forgiving one another [readily and freely], just as God in Christ also forgave you." Ephesians 4:31-32 AMP

Garbage in our lives will drain us. Just as clutter can overwhelm a physical space, allowing trash to accumulate in our lives can deeply affect our emotional, mental, physical, and, yes, even spiritual walk. As the Scriptures admonish, it's important to let go of bitterness, wrath, anger, and the perpetual animosity that can take root in our hearts. Just as clutter can consume physical spaces, these negative emotions can clutter our minds and souls. Instead, Scripture urges us to be kind and helpful to one another, to be tenderhearted and understanding. It calls us to forgive one another readily and freely, just as God in Christ forgave us. By embracing this wisdom, we can free ourselves from the burden of emotional and spiritual "garbage" and live in peace and harmony with God and others.

Initially, the effects of emotional baggage may be subtle and hard to notice. However, these effects can take on different forms, such as toxic relationships, unhealthy habits, negative thought patterns, or unfulfilling pursuits. Though we may try to bury or ignore them at first, we often underestimate their importance until they accumulate and begin to significantly interfere with our lives. Consequently, they become a heavy burden that depletes our energy and obstructs our ability to grow and thrive in our relationship with the Lord.

Much like how an unkept garden in bad soil can stifle the growth of beautiful flowers, holding onto emotional baggage and unnecessary burdens can prevent you from growing in the Lord. The longer you allow this garbage to remain, the harder it becomes to clear it away and the greater its impact on your life.

It's essential to recognize and eliminate these sources of garbage from your life. Begin by identifying the aspects that bring negativity, sadness, or anxiety, and take small but deliberate steps to dispose of them. This process may require courage and determination, but it will liberate you from the weight holding you back. We have the Holy Spirit ready and willing to show you. We only need to ask Him.

While we often recognize and address significant issues in our lives, what about the smaller ones? Sometimes, I admit that little things can bother me a lot. For example, if my husband leaves his shoes out instead of putting them away, it irritates me. And if I trip over them in the dark, then I get mad. I could just mention it when I first saw the shoes, but often, I let that irritation lead to anger, and if I continue in that anger, it will lead to a lot of other things he has done that makes the anger grow. So, what can I do to adjust my attitude? And why should I have to change how I feel? Because I am to imitate my heavenly Father and walk in love Ephesians 5:2.

If I keep on stewing about it, that will only cause the anger to grow bigger and bigger. Instead, I need to stop and give it over to the Lord right away by telling Him I am frustrated and getting angry. I could do this through a simple prayer, such as 'Lord, I am feeling frustrated and angry about this situation. I give it to you and ask for your guidance and peace, in Jesus' name.'

I allow myself to feel my feelings but under the control of my heavenly Father's guidance. I repent for my shortcomings of being easily irritated and ask for His help to show me how to rid myself of this problem of irritation and anger. I ask Him to help me change myself.

The earlier I catch myself in my irritation and turn to God, the easier it will be to control my feelings. If I continue to be irritated for a long time, it will become harder to control because it will turn into anger. I may have to ask for God's help many times, and that's okay because it is a process for me. I am working on getting rid of trash the best I can, and God is okay with that.

Also, release grudges and forgive those who have caused you pain, not for their sake, but for your spiritual growth so that it will not hinder your relationship with God. Recognize the toxic patterns in your life and replace them with constructive and nurturing ones. As you let go of the garbage, you'll notice a transformation in your outlook on life. You'll feel renewed clarity and purpose like a fresh breeze cleansing a stuffy room.

The more we allow the Holy Spirit to declutter our lives the more room you will have for the Father in heaven. Freeing ourselves from that burden of garbage in our lives will allow us to flourish and embrace the fullness of our spiritual potential. Remember that through Christ, you now have the ability to decide what you allow in your life, so choose wisely and let go of the garbage.

"For His divine power has bestowed on us [absolutely] everything necessary for [a dynamic spiritual] life and godliness, through true and personal knowledge of Him who called us by His own glory and excellence." 2 Peter 1:3 AMP

"But now you yourselves are to put off all these: anger, wrath, malice, blasphemy, filthy language out of your mouth." Colossians 3:8

Some things will be easier than others to eliminate from your life. However, things like bitterness and unforgiveness can linger and will block your spiritual walk and growth. It will hinder your hearing from the Holy Spirit. What do you do when you're hurt or when betrayal runs so deep you can't feel anything else? Especially if your anger is justified and you think you have every right not to forgive that person or persons. This verse in Matthew always made me feel uneasy:

"Then Peter came to Jesus and asked, 'Lord, how many times shall I forgive my brother when he sins against me? Up to seven times?' Jesus answered, 'I tell you, not seven times, but seventy-seven times.'" Matthew 18:21-22 NIV

As someone victimized since childhood and most of my adult life, I felt entitled and justified to hold onto anger and unforgiveness. It took me years to untangle all the damage that had been done to me, and even though I always wore a smile, deep pain and resentment lingered within me. However, I eventually realized that letting go of this pain and anger was a gradual process, a gradual release of my emotions. I learned forgiveness is an act of my will to relinquish judgment to God. Forgiveness is freeing yourself from wanting the perpetrator to pay for their wrong and accepting that they may never be sorry for the pain they caused.

It was not an easy process, but it began when I surrendered even a little bit to God, blocking the enemy and allowing the Holy Spirit to begin my healing process. Through this process, I learned that forgiving doesn't erase emotional damage overnight, but it is a necessary step to breaking free from the chains of pain.

These words of Jesus are very true: "Jesus replied, 'I tell you the truth, everyone who sins is a slave of sin' " John 8:34 NLT.

These words struck a chord within me, showing the truth of the fundamental choice we face—to either follow Jesus or become enslaved by persistent chains of sin.

The clutter of sin and negative emotions can enslave us, preventing us from reaching our full potential. So just as the Scriptures admonish, it's crucial to let go of the burdens of sin and negativity and embrace a path that leads to forgiveness, kindness, and understanding, allowing us to break free from those chains that bind us and find true spiritual liberation.

In this process, the guidance of the Holy Spirit is invaluable. He is always present and ready to help, but we must be willing to seek His help actively. By asking for His guidance, we invite Him to reveal the obstacles blocking our faith walk. These obstacles can take various forms, such as negative habits, addictions, unresolved anger, deep-seated fear, lingering resentment, destructive pride, or other sinful behaviors.

Naming and addressing these hindrances may be difficult, but it is essential for spiritual growth. The Holy Spirit is a gentle but powerful guide, leading us to face the areas of our lives that need transformation. As we recognize these negative aspects, we can begin removing them from our hearts and minds.

However, this process is not a one-time event. Just as trash can accumulate again after cleaning, some things we thought we had dealt with may creep back into our lives. Understanding that this is a natural part of the journey is crucial. Spiritual growth is an ongoing process; sometimes, we may have to address the same issues multiple times before seeing even a little transformation.

In times when we are frustrated and discouraged, we should not give up. Clearing our lives and hearts for a deeper relationship with God is of immeasurable worth. It's a treasure of great price, and our efforts in this pursuit will not be in vain. The freedom and joy that come from a closer fellowship with our Lord and Savior will make all the challenges and persistence worthwhile.

So let's be persistent in seeking the Holy Spirit's guidance, allowing Him to help us identify and remove any trash that obstructs our path to spiritual growth. Let us embrace this journey of transformation, knowing that each step we take brings us closer to the abundant life God intends for us. As we continue to clear the way for the King of Kings in our lives, we will experience the beauty of His love and the richness of His presence in ways we could never imagine. Our heavenly Father promises His help and healing. From your deepest pit, His arm will lift you out.

"He heals the brokenhearted and binds up their wounds." Psalm 147:3

Dear Lord,

The Refuse Gate represents the debris and obstacles on my path to spiritual growth. I come before You with a humble heart.

Make me aware of anything blocking my journey or chains that may be holding and binding me.

Holy Spirit, I seek Your help to shine light in the dark places of my life. Teach me to clear away the rubble and remove anything that hinders Your truth from living within me. I surrender these areas to Your cleansing power, trusting in Your life-changing grace.

In Jesus' name, I pray, amen.

# CHAPTER 6
# SUMMARY OF THE FIRST FIVE GATES

"Then Judah said, 'The strength of the laborers is failing, and there is so much rubbish that we are not able to build the wall.'"
Nehemiah 4:10

The first five gates serve as the foundation for building the walls and closing off certain aspects of our lives. We progress from salvation through the Sheep Gate, to sharing our faith and growing through the Fish Gate, to leaving behind our old selves through the Old Gate, overcoming trials by focusing on Jesus through the Valley Gate, and getting rid of anything that hinders our spiritual growth through the Refuse Gate.

Building this foundation is a challenging task that requires consistent effort. As the Scripture in Nehemiah 4:10 suggests, this work can seem overwhelming and drain our strength, leaving us feeling weak and discouraged.

Nehemiah looked to God and said just a quick, short prayer, "strengthen my hands!" Nehemiah 6:9. This short little prayer, said in faith, is powerful! God never wants us to be alone; our heavenly Father desires to be our constant companion. We succeed through His strength and wisdom, but we must ask and believe God for it.

Turning to Jesus is the only way to gain a new perspective and strength when you feel hopeless and helpless. People can only help or listen for a little while and, at best, give a little sympathy. The Holy Spirit has the answers you need, though it may not be a quick fix. We all want an immediate response, but growth and maturity take time. A day-to-day relationship with our Father takes time.

Faith is built through a gradual process of trusting in God and His Word over time. But unforgiveness, bitterness, and doubt will block our progress and stunt our growth. We will continue to move forward if we are at least willing to allow the Holy Spirit to search us and show us where we are blocked. If we are always trying to surrender each day, we will grow even if it does not feel like we are.

Circumstances, trauma, and people may have torn down the walls of your life, and the gates may have been destroyed with fire, but with God's help through Jesus, you can rebuild. We can be sure of this because the Scriptures tell us it is so. The Word says he knew us before we were formed:

"You made all the delicate, inner parts of my body and knit me together in my mother's womb. Thank you for making me so wonderfully complex! Your workmanship is marvelous—how well I know it. You watched me as I was being formed in utter seclusion, as I was woven together in the dark of the womb. You saw me before I was born. Every day of my life was recorded in your book. Every moment was laid out before a single day had passed." Psalm 139:13-16

God's promise to take care of us always is a comforting thought that brings hope and reassurance. It means that no matter what challenges we might face in life, we can trust in God's love and protection. This promise reminds us that we are not alone and can rely on God's strength and guidance to get us through difficult times. It reminds us that we are valuable and precious to God, and His care for us is eternal.

"I will be your God throughout your lifetime- until your hair is white with age. I made you, and I will care for you. I will carry you along and save you." Isaiah 46:4 NLT

Our heavenly Father desires to take care of us and build us up, while the enemy comes in to wreak havoc and destruction in our lives by destroying our walls and burning our gates: "The thief does not come except to steal, and to kill, and to destroy." John 10:10

God wants to help us rebuild those walls, hang those gates back up in our lives, and restore us to where He intended us to be in His kingdom. Amid life's trials and challenges, we can find comfort in our heavenly Father's desire to care for and support us through every difficulty. Like a loving and compassionate parent, He yearns to see us flourish and grow, offering guidance and reassurance when we feel lost or broken. His ultimate desire is to rebuild the broken parts of our lives and restore us to a state of strength and abundance.

However, our adversary wants to sow chaos and destruction in our lives. This enemy aims to break down the healthy walls we want around our hearts and minds, erode our defenses, and weaken our spirits. Just like a vicious invader, the enemy uses various tactics to wreak havoc on our emotional, physical, mental, and spiritual well-being, leaving us feeling vulnerable and defeated.

When we are distressed, it can feel as though our walls have crumbled and our gates have been set ablaze, leaving us defenseless against the onslaught of adversity. The enemy's destructive actions may result in self-doubt, fear, bitterness, or despair, overwhelming us and hindering our progress in life. Yet despite these trials, we can find hope in the promise of our heavenly Father's unwavering love and protection. He stands ready to help us rebuild what has been torn apart, mend what has been shattered, and reignite the flames of resilience and courage within us.

With His divine strength and guidance, we can rise from the ashes, more determined than ever before. Though the enemy may try to tear us down, we can draw upon the faith and assurance that our heavenly Father is always by our side, offering a steady hand to lead us out of darkness into the light.

Through prayer, reflection, and seeking His guidance, we can fortify our walls with the power of love, forgiveness, and perseverance, making it harder for the enemy's destructive influences to penetrate our lives. In this ongoing battle between God's divine care and Satan's destructive forces, we have the power, through Christ, to choose which one will ultimately prevail in our lives. By embracing our heavenly Father's love and allowing Him to rebuild and strengthen us, we can stand firm against the storms of life and emerge victorious over the enemy's attempts to bring havoc and destruction into our lives. In unity with our heavenly Father, we can rebuild our walls, reignite our hope, and find solace in knowing that we are never alone on this walk through life.

Through this study, our goal is to uncover insights that we can personally apply to healing and spiritual growth in our lives. Now let's continue our exploration together as we investigate the significance of the next five gates in Nehemiah.

# CHAPTER 7
# THE FOUNTAIN GATE

"Shallun the son of Col-Hozeh, leader of the district of Mizpah, repaired the Fountain Gate; he built it, covered it, hung its doors with its bolts and bars, and repaired the wall of the Pool of Shelah by the King's Garden, as far as the stairs that go down from the City of David."

Nehemiah 3:15

The Fountain Gate was so named because it was the access to the Gihon Spring, Jerusalem's sole source of life-giving water available all year round. In the same way, we need God's Holy Spirit to be our only source of living water. The Fountain Gate is located after the Refuse Gate. I believe this is intentional as it symbolizes that as we clean the trash out of our lives and allow true faith to replace it, the fountains begin to flow, and the living waters of the Holy Spirit cleanse our lives and empower us for our Christian walk.

As we consider the symbolism behind the Fountain Gate and its connection to the life-giving waters of the Gihon Spring, it echoes a deep spiritual truth about Christ as our living water. In this Scripture, Jesus invites us with open arms as He proclaims, "If anyone thirsts, let him come to Me and drink."

"On the last day, that great day of the feast, Jesus stood and cried out, saying, 'If anyone thirsts, let him come to Me and drink. He who believes in Me, as the Scripture has said, out of his heart will flow rivers of living water.' But this He spoke concerning the Spirit, whom those believing in Him would receive; for the Holy Spirit was not yet given because Jesus was not yet glorified." John 7:37-39

This invitation is a powerful reminder there is living water available to us through Christ. The Fountain Gate, strategically positioned after the Refuse Gate, mirrors how we rid ourselves of what hinders our spiritual walk and fill ourselves up with His Word. Just as the fountains are made to flow when the trash is cleared, our lives are purified and empowered by the living waters of the Holy Spirit.

However, if, as Christians, we choose to live according to our desires and disregard God's instructions laid out in the Bible to live our lives in accordance with the teachings of Christ, then we are committing two evils as this Scripture warns us: "For My people have committed *two evils*; they have forsaken Me, the Fountain of living waters, to hew out cisterns for themselves, broken cisterns that can hold no water" Jeremiah 2:13.

What are the two evils they committed? The first evil was they had forsaken God, the fountain of life.

Jesus answered and said to her, "Whoever drinks of this water will thirst again, but whoever drinks of the water that I shall give him will never thirst. But the water that I shall give him will become in him a fountain of water springing up into everlasting life" John 4:13-14.

In the above scripture in John, Jesus speaks of the temporary nature of earthly water and contrasts it with the everlasting life-giving water He offers. "Whoever drinks of the water that I shall give him will never thirst," He promises, "but the water that I shall give him will become in him a fountain of water springing up into everlasting life."

This insightful truth illustrates our deep need for Jesus, the living water, to sustain us spiritually. When we turn away in doubt and disbelief of His promises and decide to go our way without God, we are forsaking our source of life.

Forsaking God is a significant and weighty decision that will affect our lives and spiritual well-being. The belief in Jesus as the living water, used in the Bible to represent the spiritual water and nourishment He provides, underscores God's essential role in our lives.

In embracing Jesus as the living water, we acknowledge that our souls thirst for something deeper and greater than the material world can provide. We recognize that true fulfillment and contentment come from a relationship with God, who offers unconditional love, grace, and purpose. Just as water sustains physical life, Jesus sustains our spiritual lives, offering the comfort, guidance, and strength needed for life's challenges.

When we turn away from God, we risk severing this vital connection with our source of life. Doubt is a natural part of faith, but when we allow it to overpower our trust in God's promises, we may drift away from the path He has laid out for us. It becomes tempting to rely solely on ourselves with our limited understanding, making decisions without seeking His guidance.

Forsaking God goes beyond denying religious beliefs. It means turning away from God's love and wisdom that can bring fulfillment to our lives and positively impact those around us. It can lead to feelings of loneliness, emptiness, and a sense of being adrift in the world without purpose or direction.

When we decide to go our way without God, we risk falling into self-reliance, pride, and selfishness. We may become entangled in worldly pursuits and material possessions, believing they will bring lasting happiness. We will find that the joy derived from such pursuits is often fleeting and shallow, leaving us thirsting for something more meaningful.

The decision to forsake God also carries spiritual consequences. It can lead to a hardening of the heart, making it more challenging to reconnect with our faith and rediscover the path to God's presence. The Bible refers to this hardening as the heart being "as fat as grease." "Their heart is as fat as grease, But I delight in Your law" Psalm 119:70.

Yet it's essential to remember that God's love is ever-present, and His forgiveness is boundless. Even in moments of doubt or disbelief, we can find our way back to Him through sincere repentance and a willingness to rekindle our relationship with Jesus.

Embracing Jesus as the Living Water means acknowledging that our lives find their true purpose and fulfillment in divine communion. It means recognizing that we are not meant to travel through this life alone but with the guiding hand of a loving and compassionate creator God. By staying connected to our source of life, we can draw from an infinite wellspring of love, grace, and wisdom to sustain us through all life's challenges and joys.

The second evil was, the people made cisterns for themselves apart from God. Cisterns and wells serve different purposes, and it may be helpful to differentiate between the two. A well functions as a source of water in and of itself, while a cistern is designed to store water from an external source.

The people turned to idols and trusted in themselves, so their artificial cistern was broken and unable to hold water. The Lord says those who trust in their own resources are like broken cisterns, unable to hold the living water of the Holy Spirit in their lives.

At some point in our lives, we may come across a critical situation where we have to make crucial decisions about the path we choose to take. In such a situation, it is essential to embrace and follow the teachings in the Word of God. Clinging to His Word will help us align ourselves with the marvelous restoration brought about by Christ's redemptive love, enabling us to embody the new man, transformed and reborn in the image of our Savior.

In diverting our focus away from God and indulging in self-centered pursuits, we turn our backs on His unyielding love and guidance, creating a chasm between ourselves and our heavenly source of all that is good and righteous. In these distancing moments, we risk weakening our connection with our almighty Father, leaving us vulnerable and spiritually thirsty.

It is important to constantly remind ourselves of the responsibility we have to embrace our heavenly Father's precious Word. We are not just passive recipients of God's grace but active participants in a divine covenant. This sacred partnership requires us to seek the path of righteousness and spiritual growth continuously. By doing so, we ensure that God's infinite wisdom and compassion flow freely within us, sustaining our souls and nurturing our relationship with Him.

As believers in Christ, we should relentlessly endeavor to cling to His teachings and live according to the new person He has made us to be. Let's reject the temptation of self-centeredness, accept His Word, and firmly follow the righteous path that leads to eternal satisfaction, knowing that our loving God embraces us with His unwavering love and grace.

But Nehemiah's journey to the Fountain Gate unveiled a sobering reality—the path was so blocked that he couldn't get through.

"Then I went on to the Fountain Gate and to the King's Pool, but there was no room for the animal under me to pass" Nehemiah 2:14.

The Fountain Gate appears to be the gate that was in the most ruin. The path had so much rubble that it completely blocked Nehemiah's way, and he could not pass. Have we built our own broken, useless cisterns and blocked the Holy Spirit so He cannot work in us?

In order to determine whether we have blocked the Holy Spirit, we must first understand His role in our lives and what functions He serves. Although the Holy Spirit may seem mysterious and elusive at times, He is actually an essential component of our Christian growth. Unfortunately, we often fail to recognize His presence because we are unfamiliar with Him.

How can we grow closer to the Holy Spirit and learn to listen to His guidance? The Holy Spirit desires to communicate with us on a daily basis, which means we should be familiar with the ways He operates. When we understand how He works, it becomes easier to recognize His leading. Here are some of the ways the Holy Spirit might grab our attention. As you go about your day and study the Word, keep an eye out for these signs and see if you experience any of them. Here are just a few ways the Holy Spirit ministers to us:

## HE DWELLS IN US

"Do you not know that you are the temple of God and that the Spirit of God dwells in you?" 1 Corinthians 3:16

There is an intimate relationship between believers and the Holy Spirit. The idea of being a temple implies a continuous indwelling of God's presence within us. Understanding this indwelling presence transforms the way we live by empowering, guiding, and comforting us on our journey of faith. It invites us to walk in humility and gratitude, recognizing that we are vessels of God's love and instruments of His grace in the world.

This understanding changes how we approach challenges by relying on prayer, seeking God's guidance, and surrendering our will to His divine purpose. The continuous indwelling of the Holy Spirit becomes a source of resilience, joy, and purpose, shaping our lives into a living testimony of God's life-altering love.

If you're seeking to be more aware of God's presence in your daily life, try asking Him to make His presence known to you. Work on cultivating that awareness over time and see if you notice a growing sense of closeness to God, as well as an increasing awareness of His guidance in your life.

## HE TEACHES US BY REVEALING THE SCRIPTURES TO US

"But the Helper, the Holy Spirit, whom the Father will send in My name, He will teach you all things, and bring to your remembrance all things that I said to you" John 14:26.

The Holy Spirit will help us understand the Scriptures, unveiling spiritual truths beyond mere intellectual knowledge. It is a personalized encounter with God's wisdom that brings relevance to our journeys. The Spirit reveals the profound truths, principles, and promises in the Word. This scripture tells us that the Holy Spirit teaches and reminds us of Christ's teachings. This teaching ministry is an ongoing revelation that deepens our understanding of God.

Before reading the Bible, seek the guidance of the Holy Spirit and ask for insights to deepen your understanding of biblical truths and their practical application in your life.

## HE STRENGTHENS US

"I pray that from his glorious, unlimited resources he will empower you with inner strength through His Spirit" Ephesians 3:16 NLT.

Ephesians unveils a profound aspect of the Holy Spirit's ministry—His role in strengthening us. This "inner strength" is a resilience that fortifies our spirits beyond physical or emotional endurance. It isn't a superficial or temporary empowerment; it draws from the boundless resources of God's glory. It is a beautiful gift the Holy Spirit uses to transform weakness into resilience and fear into courage.

The Holy Spirit serves as our anchor during times of difficulty. He provides us with unwavering support and access to God's abundant strength. This knowledge instills confidence in us, enabling us to face challenges head-on while relying on His power and expressing our thanks for His unending resources.

Reflect on your ability to face challenges with resilience. Ask for strength when you feel weak or overwhelmed. Look for increased perseverance, courage, and the ability to overcome challenges.

## HE BRINGS US FREEDOM

"Now the Lord is the Spirit, and where the Spirit of the Lord is, there is freedom" 2 Corinthians 3:17 NLT.

The Holy Spirit brings true freedom that aligns with God's perfect will and leads to a fulfilling life. This freedom liberates the soul from sin, guilt, and condemnation, allowing us to walk in the light of God's grace. We should let go of fear, doubt, and self-reliance and seek the Holy Spirit's guidance. As we yield to the life-changing work of the Holy Spirit, we experience a freedom that surpasses earthly limitations and finds its foundation in the eternal truths of God's love and grace.

Take some time to think about areas in your life where you may feel limited or restrained. It's worth considering whether the choices you make and the things you do align with the principles of God's Word. Ask the Holy Spirit to help you identify areas where you need freedom, and pray for the Holy Spirit's guidance to break any chains that may be holding you back. You might also want to explore some Bible verses that discuss freedom and investigate the role of the Holy Spirit in bringing liberation to your life.

## HE ASSURES US THAT WE BELONG TO CHRIST

"The Spirit Himself bears witness with our spirit that we are children of God" Romans 8:16.

This personal confirmation is based on God's recognition that we are His children, not on our merits or achievements. The Spirit testifies to our adoption into God's family, creating a firm foundation for our identities. This assurance offers comfort and security, empowering us to approach God with confidence and gratitude. It transforms how we view ourselves and the world around us, fostering a deep sense of purpose and belonging in the arms of our loving heavenly Father.

When feeling unsure of your identity as a child of God, seek reassurance from the Holy Spirit through God's Word to deepen your sense of security and confidence in your relationship with God.

## HE EMPOWERS US TO SPEAK BOLDLY OF CHRIST

"And when they had prayed, the place where they were assembled together was shaken; and they were all filled with the Holy Spirit, and they spoke the word of God with boldness" Acts 4:31.

This verse in Acts shows the Holy Spirit empowering believers to speak boldly about Christ. This divine enablement goes beyond natural abilities and transforms timid hearts into courageous vessels of proclamation. It is available to all believers who seek the Spirit's filling through prayer and surrender. This empowerment makes us bold to speak truth in love, face challenges with confidence, and become effective ambassadors for Christ.

Evaluate your willingness to share your faith. Pray for courage and effectiveness in speaking about Christ and sharing the gospel.

## THE HOLY SPIRIT WANTS TO TRANSFORM US TO BE LIKE CHRIST

"But the fruit of the Spirit is love, joy, peace, forbearance, kindness, goodness, faithfulness, gentleness and self-control. Against such things there is no law" Galatians 5:22-23.

Galatians teaches us that the Holy Spirit can transform our lives by cultivating virtues that reflect Christ's character. Surrendering to the Spirit's work allows us to experience a liberating journey toward Christlikeness, producing a living testimony to the transforming power of God's love. As we cooperate with the Spirit, we become conduits of Christ's character, reflecting His light and love to a world in need of redemption.

Take a moment to reflect on your life and see if it reflects the "fruit of the Spirit": love, joy, peace, patience, kindness, goodness, faithfulness, gentleness, and self-control. Ask for the Holy Spirit's guidance and He will grow these Christlike virtues in your life. Remember that developing these qualities takes time and effort, just like a craftsman hones their skills through dedication and repetition. The Holy Spirit works within us, shaping and molding our character over time. By inviting the Holy Spirit into our lives, He will gradually transform us to become more Christlike. Each step forward brings us closer to the fullness of who we are meant to be. So, be patient and trust in God's transforming power.

Looking for these workings of the Holy Spirit involves an ongoing journey of spiritual awareness and growth. Regular self-reflection, sincere prayer, and a willingness to cooperate with the Holy Spirit are essential elements in recognizing and experiencing the life-changing power of God in your life.

It is also a good idea to stop during your day, thank the Holy Spirit for being there, and ask Him to help you hear and know Him better. As you continue to practice listening to the Holy Spirit, you will become more sensitive to His voice. However, it is important to remember that this will take time and effort. It is all part of your personal growth as a soldier of Christ. The Lord is training you to be effective in His army, and just like any other training, it requires patience and perseverance. Therefore, please don't be too hard on yourself; our heavenly Father has boundless patience and will never tire of you.

It is important to keep in mind that the Holy Spirit is the Spirit of truth, and His voice will never contradict God's Word. So if you ever question whether or not you have heard from the Lord, always remember that His message must align with His Word.

This gate also mentions that it had bolts and bars. That could remind us that the Holy Spirit is the One who brings the Word alive to us and guards the treasure that dwells in us. It also reminds us that His Holy Spirit seals us.

"Through the power of the Holy Spirit who lives within us, carefully guard the precious truth that has been entrusted to you" 2 Timothy 1:14 NLT.

"In Him you also trusted, after you heard the word of truth, the gospel of your salvation; in whom also, having believed, you were sealed with the Holy Spirit of promise" Ephesians 1:13.

Were you aware we can grieve the Holy Spirit?

"And do not grieve the Holy Spirit of God, by whom you are sealed until the day of redemption" Ephesians 4:30.

The Greek word used for "grieve" in this context implies causing emotional distress or sorrow. This passage emphasizes the personhood of the Holy Spirit. By understanding this, we can grasp the gravity of our actions and attitudes that may displease or sadden the Holy Spirit. One primary way we grieve the Holy Spirit is by failing to crucify our fleshly desires and impulses.

The Christian walk involves continually striving to align our lives with the teachings of Christ, working to overcome our selfish desires and sinful natures. When we yield to anger, lust, envy, or other ungodly emotions without restraint, we quench the work of the Holy Spirit in our lives. Even if we have been hurt or wronged, the Holy Spirit calls us to forgive and release our hurts, justified or not, to God rather than dwelling in bitterness or seeking revenge. Holding on to resentment hinders our spiritual growth and inhibits the Spirit's life-changing work in us.

Another way we can grieve the Holy Spirit is by resisting the Word of God. The Scriptures teach us how to live righteously and provide divine wisdom for our daily choices. When we intentionally disregard or reject God's Word, we show a lack of trust and submission to the Holy Spirit's guidance. To walk out our Christian faith effectively, we must be attentive to the leading of the Holy Spirit and cultivate a relationship with God through prayer, worship, and the study of His Word. As we surrender to God's will and allow the Spirit to work in us, we experience spiritual growth and are empowered to live a life that honors God and reflects His love for people.

Grieving the Holy Spirit can happen when we neglect to crucify our fleshly desires, harbor unforgiveness, or resist the guidance of God's Word. Recognizing the personhood of the Holy Spirit and His desire to lead us into righteousness should motivate us to want a deeper relationship with God, allowing the Spirit to shape our lives and transform us into the image of Christ.

Many Scriptures teach us how to live in a way that is pleasing to God. Here is just one from Ephesians:

"With the Lord's authority I say this: Live no longer as the Gentiles do, for they are hopelessly confused. Their minds are full of darkness; they wander far from the life God gives because they have closed their minds and hardened their hearts against him. They have no sense of shame. They live for lustful pleasure and eagerly practice every kind of impurity. But that isn't what you learned about Christ. Since you have heard about Jesus and have learned the truth that comes from him, throw off your old sinful nature and your former way of life, which is corrupted by lust and deception. Instead, let the Spirit renew your thoughts and attitudes. Put on your new nature, created to be like God—truly righteous and holy. So stop telling lies. Let us tell our neighbors the truth, for we are all parts of the same body. And 'Don't sin by letting anger control you.' Don't let the sun go down while you are still angry, for anger gives a foothold to the devil. If you are a thief, quit stealing. Instead, use your hands for good hard work and give generously to others in need. Don't use foul or abusive language. Let everything you say be good and helpful, so that your words will be an encouragement to those who hear them. And do not bring sorrow to God's Holy Spirit by the way you live. Remember, he has identified you as his own, guaranteeing that you will be saved on the day of redemption. Get rid of all bitterness, rage, anger, harsh words, slander, as well as all types of evil behavior. Instead, be kind to each other, tenderhearted, forgiving one another, just as God through Christ has forgiven you" Ephesians 4:17-32 NLT.

Can we do this perfectly? No, of course not. However, what matters is if we consistently strive to live out our faith, acknowledge our poor choices by repenting, and seek the Holy Spirit to fill us with His abundant blessings every day.

At the Fountain Gate, we experience the flow of living water from within us as the Holy Spirit empowers us. This gate reveals how the Holy Spirit moves through our lives, producing fruit and enabling us to excel in every good work. The Holy Spirit illuminates specific passages that speak to our hearts when we read God's Word.

There is a warning for us when we continually refuse to move forward in our Christian walk and instead look back at Egypt and want to return to our old ways:

"They refused to obey, And they were not mindful of Your wonders That You did among them. But they hardened their necks, And in their rebellion, They appointed a leader To return to their bondage. But You are God, Ready to pardon, Gracious and merciful, Slow to anger, Abundant in kindness, and did not forsake them" Nehemiah 9:17.

"But Jesus said to him, 'No one, having put his hand to the plow, and looking back, is fit for the kingdom of God'" Luke 9:62.

As we move toward healing and restoration, we must avoid the temptation to return to Egypt by looking back to the past, which will keep us in bondage. If we put our hand on the plow, we must continue to move forward. If we miss it, and we will, He is always there, ready to forgive us when we ask Him. Let's follow the path of Christ and take each step with faith and trust in Him.

We are privileged to partner with the Holy Spirit, who will work powerfully in and through our lives. On this journey to be whole, let it be our goal to be faithful to His Word and make our heavenly Father proud.

Precious heavenly Father,

Thank You for the living water flowing through my life. Today, I come before you with a heart of gratitude for the refreshing streams of Your love and grace. Lord, reveal to me any cisterns of self-centered waters that I have built. Grant me the strength to demolish these barriers and let Your living water cleanse my soul.

Show me where I may be blocked and need freedom. Open my eyes to recognize the gentle whispers of the Holy Spirit, guiding me on the path of righteousness. I surrender my will to You, trusting in Your perfect plan for my life. Help me clear away the rubble of doubts, fears, and distractions so that I can grow and the fruits of the Spirit will be evident in my life.

Grant me the courage to move forward, leaving behind the things of the past. May Your living water continue to flow in and through me, bringing life and abundance.

In Jesus' name, I pray, amen.

# CHAPTER 8

# THE WATER GATE

"Moreover the Nethinim who dwelt in Ophel made repairs as far as the place in front of the Water Gate toward the east, and on the projecting tower."
Nehemiah 3:26

In the previous chapter, we learned about the Fountain Gate, which had important access to the Gihon Spring—the source of life-giving water. Unlike many other cities, Jerusalem was not built near a river and had to rely on reservoirs and the Gihon Spring to meet its water needs. The Fountain Gate was located next to the Water Gate. I believe that the proximity of the Fountain Gate to the Water Gate is not accidental but rather has a deliberate spiritual connection. The Water Gate symbolizes the power of the living Word of God, which the Holy Spirit (Fountain Gate) makes alive for us individually, bringing cleansing, encouragement, and direction to our lives. The reading of the Law was held at the Water Gate to all who could hear and understand.

"Now all the people gathered together as one man in the open square that was in front of the Water Gate; and they told Ezra the scribe, to bring the Book of the Law of Moses, which the Lord had commanded Israel. So Ezra the priest brought the Law before the assembly of men and women and all who could hear with understanding on the first day of the seventh month. Then he read from it in the open square that was in front of the Water Gate from morning until midday, before the men and women and those who could understand; and the ears of all the people were attentive to the Book of the Law"Nehemiah 8:1-3.

The people gathered to hear the Word of God read to them. They stood on their feet and listened attentively to it, showing great respect for the Law. They stood there from daylight to midday. They wanted to hear and understand. Verse nine says all the people wept when they listened to the Book of the Law. We are encouraged in the same way today by the New Testament words of Jesus to listen and learn from His Word.

"But He answered and said, 'It is written, "Man shall not live by bread alone, but by every word that proceeds out of the mouth of God"' Matthew 4:4.

We need to grow in our walk with the Father and pay close attention to His Word by reading, studying, and meditating on it. The more we do, the more spiritual understanding the Holy Spirit will give us. But if we profess that we know the Word without really experiencing a relationship with the Father and are disinterested in His teachings, then even what we think we know will be taken away. We have a great treasure and responsibility to learn God's Word, which He has given us, and we should never take it lightly.

"Then he added, 'Pay close attention to what you hear. The closer you listen, the more my teaching, more understanding will be given. But for those who are not listening, even what little understanding they have will be taken away from them' " Mark 4:24-25 NLT.

Hearing and reading God's Word is essential to the Christian life. Through the Scriptures, believers learn about God's character, His will for us, and the redemptive work of Jesus Christ. However, as crucial as it is to engage with the Word, the life-changing power of the Scriptures only becomes fruitful when it is paired with action.

The Bible repeatedly emphasizes the importance of applying God's teachings in our lives. In the book of James, it says:

"For if you listen to the Word and don't obey, it is like glancing at your face in a mirror. You see yourself, walk away, and forget what you look like. But if you look carefully into the perfect law that sets you free, and if you do what it says and don't forget what you heard, then God will bless you for doing it" James 1:23-25 NLT.

This passage emphasizes the risk of simply being a passive listener of God's Word. If we do not act upon our received teachings, we deceive ourselves, and our being transformed will remain unattained. The analogy of looking into a mirror and immediately forgetting one's reflection illustrates how ineffective it is to hear or read the Word without applying it to our lives.

Following God's Word requires obedience and alignment with His principles. As we internalize the Scriptures and allow them to shape our thoughts, attitudes, and behaviors, we begin to walk in God's ways and live according to His will and purpose. Furthermore, Jesus emphasized the significance of obedience in His teachings. In Matthew 7:24-27, He shares the parable of the wise and foolish builders. A wise builder hears Jesus' words and acts on them, while a foolish builder hears the words but does not put them into practice. When the storms of life come, only the house built on a solid foundation rooted in obedience to God's Word stands strong.

In Ephesians 4:1-2, Jesus urges believers to "live a life worthy of the calling [they] have received." This means we should demonstrate humility, gentleness, patience, and love in our daily lives. When we base our actions on the Word of God, we align ourselves with His will and become instruments of His love and grace in the world. Our faith becomes tangible, and we become living testimonies of God's life-altering power. As we obey and apply His teachings, we grow in spiritual maturity and experience the blessings and freedom promised to those who follow His ways.

While God's Word is vital to our walk of faith, the practical application of His teachings brings about genuine transformation in our lives. Obedience to God's Word leads to a life that reflects His love, truth, and righteousness, impacting ourselves and the world around us. Through hearing and doing, we live out the Christian faith and fulfill our calling to be Christ's ambassadors in a broken world.

"But don't just listen to God's word. You must do what it says. Otherwise, you are only fooling yourselves" James 1:22 NLT.

So how important is it that we become doers of the Word? Why should we take the seed that was implanted in our souls at salvation and cultivate and water it? The Bible tells us we must have faith to please God:

"Now the just shall live by faith; But if anyone draws back, My soul has no pleasure in him" Hebrews 10:38.

But what exactly is faith according to the Word?

"Now faith is the assurance (title deed, confirmation) of things hoped for (divinely guaranteed), and the evidence of things not seen [the conviction of their reality--faith comprehends as fact what cannot be experienced by the physical senses]" Hebrews 11:1 AMP.

Faith believes that what we are hoping for will happen even

if we can't see the fulfillment of it now. That's some strong faith. The Word even tells us that we cannot please God if we don't have that kind of faith.

"But without faith it is impossible to please Him, for he who comes to God must believe that He is, and that He is a rewarder of those who diligently seek Him" Hebrews 11:6.

I know I'm not the only one who has experienced moments of doubt in their faith. Have you ever felt like you lack faith at times? Hebrews 11 lists several people the Lord considered to have significant faith, such as Abraham, Moses, Joseph, and Enoch. I don't know about you, but I would never consider myself in the same category as Moses or Abraham. How could I believe like Moses, whose faith parted the Red Sea?

One day, however, as I read this passage, the Holy Spirit gave me a completely different view of this faith list. As I read Hebrews 11 now, I no longer skim over it, feeling uncomfortable that I don't have an Abraham kind of faith. Now it encourages me!

What made the difference? Well, this time, it wasn't the great works they did that caught my attention. First, the name of Sarah, Abraham's wife, jumped out at me in verse 11.

There are a couple of things that stand out to me when I think of Sarah. One is that the Bible mentions she was beautiful, and second, in Genesis chapter 18, she overheard God talking with Abraham about having a son, and she laughed. And when God asked her why she laughed, she *lied* and said she did not laugh. Yet here she is in Hebrews 11 with the statement that her faith gave her strength to conceive!

That made me stop and think. Then I remembered that Moses argued with God in Exodus chapter four. *He argued with God.* He did not want God to send him *anywhere* to do *anything* for *anyone*. The chapter also mentions Rahab, Gideon, Barak, Samson, and Jephthah. Let's take a quick but closer look at them:

Rahab was a prostitute Joshua 2:1.

Gideon was afraid and put out fleeces, asking God to first have one be damp with dew and the second be dry so he would have reassurance that the Lord really had chosen him Judges 6:15, 36.

Barak would only go to battle if Deborah, the prophetess, went with him Judges 4:8.

Samson had lots of character flaws Judges :14-16.

Jephthah was cast out of his family because he was an illegitimate son and lived among scoundrels. He became a judge over Israel. He vowed to God that if he were given the victory in a particular battle, he would sacrifice the first thing to meet him when he returned home, which turned out to be his daughter Judges 11:30-31.

I found it fascinating that God chose imperfect and flawed individuals as examples of incredible faith in the Bible. Despite their doubts, fears, and hasty vows, these broken people are given a place in Scripture as having great faith. I reflected on this deeply. The Bible even calls them a great cloud of witnesses.

"Therefore we also, since we are surrounded by so great a cloud of witnesses" Hebrews 12:1.

The Scripture says these people surround us who, although they were imperfect and sometimes made bad decisions, believed God's promises and are now cheering us on. I now see the "cheering" a lot differently.

What if Sarah's cheers were something like this: "Listen, I laughed at the promise of God, and then I lied about it, so keep on going! If I can make it, so can you!"

Moses might say, "I didn't want to lead the people, and I tried to tell God no; I tried to give Him all kinds of excuses as to why I wasn't the man for the job. Don't give up! God won't give up on you!"

And Gideon might say, "I was the least of the people, a nobody stuck in a valley of fear, but God used me! God even called me a mighty man of valor when I was the most afraid!"

I suddenly saw these people as having a much more realistic view of faith in the heavenly Father, and it blew me away to think He listed them in a faith chapter as examples for us. It now became easier for me to understand how to apply the next part of the verse to my life:

"Let us lay aside every weight, and the sin which so easily ensnares us, and let us run with endurance the race that is set before us, looking unto Jesus, the author and finisher of our faith" Hebrews 12:1-2.

Now I see that as an imperfect human, I can lay aside every weight (burden, load, fear, hindrance) and the sin that easily snares me. I can run my race. When I am not moving forward spiritually, I ask the Holy Spirit to show me if something is weighing me down and stopping me. Unforgiveness is a considerable weight that will burden you and keep you from moving forward. Also, whatever sin it is that easily traps you repeatedly will hinder you, too. That could be addiction, fear, anger, or anything that trips you up and stops =you from getting up and running again. We must decide how important the faith race is to us. The Word of God says to run in a way that will get you the prize.

"Do you not know that those who run in a race all run, but one receives the prize? Run in such a way that you may obtain it. And everyone who competes for the prize is temperate in all things. Now they do it to obtain a perishable crown, but we for an imperishable crown. Therefore I run thus: not with uncertainty. Thus I fight: not as one who beats the air. But I discipline my body and bring it into subjection, lest, when I have preached to others, I myself should become disqualified" 1 Corinthians 9:24-27.

When people train for a race, they discipline themselves. Whatever it takes, they will do it because they want to win. If that means getting up early every day to exercise and eat only certain foods, going to bed early, or not hanging out with friends but training instead, then that is the sacrifice they are willing to make to be in shape to win. Serious athletes dedicated to winning go all out; nothing is more important. In the same way, we must decide if we will throw off the things of this world and the weights we carry and discipline ourselves to the Word, not just as a hearer but also as a doer and run our spiritual race.

The Old Testament saints who went before us in their imperfect way are cheering us on, assuring us that we can trust God and His promises. We may trip and fall, but we have Jesus to lift us back on our feet and get us running again. And He will catch us no matter how many times it takes. We need to be willing to surrender to Him, believe Him, and get up and keep going.

My eternal race is the most important race of my life, and I want to win it. How about you?

Dear Heavenly Father,

As I reflect on the lessons learned at the Water Gate, I pray for the discipline to prioritize daily reading and hearing Your Word. Grant me the wisdom to understand and apply its teachings, making

Your Word come alive in me.

Lord, I desire to be a wise builder, constructing my life on the solid foundation of Your truth. Make me usable for Your kingdom's purposes, and may my life be a testimony to Your glory. Holy Spirit, You planted the seed of faith within me. Water it with the richness of Your Word, nurturing growth and bearing fruit in abundance.

In my spiritual race, I seek Your guidance and strength. Help me persevere, keeping my eyes fixed on You, the author and finisher of my faith.

In the powerful name of Jesus, I pray, amen!

# CHAPTER 9
# THE HORSE GATE

*"Beyond the Horse Gate the priests made repairs, each in front of his own house."*
Nehemiah 3:28

The Horse Gate may have been located near the stables that housed the horses used in battles against enemies. We saw that it was the priests who repaired the Sheep Gate, and notably, they were the ones who fixed this gate. I like to imagine Jesus, my High Priest, standing guard on the front lines of my spiritual battles. This thought is in line with the promise from 2 Thessalonians:

"But the Lord is faithful, and He will strengthen you [setting you on a firm foundation] and will protect and guard you from the evil one." 2 Thessalonians 3:3 AMP

And there is spiritual warfare in the Christian life. As believers, we are bound to encounter spiritual battles and challenges during our fight for faith. The Christian life is not always easy or without struggle. Whether we are aware or not, a spiritual battle rages around us. It involves spiritual conflicts, temptations, and obstacles that can hinder our relationship with God and the ability to live out our faith.

As Christians, we are encouraged to be aware of this battle and to equip ourselves with the necessary spiritual tools and armor to stand firm in the faith. This involves developing a solid relationship with God, studying the Bible and putting its teachings into practice, praying, relying on the power and guidance of the Holy Spirit, and surrounding yourself with fellow believers who can provide support and encouragement.

We want to be watchful and prepared for any challenge that might arise in the Christian walk. It may not always be smooth, but with determination, reliance on God, and a firm understanding of the spiritual battle, believers can overcome obstacles and grow strong in their relationships with our heavenly Father. The apostle Peter reminds us:

"Be sober, be vigilant, because your adversary the devil walks about like a roaring lion, seeking whom he may devour" 1 Peter 5:8.

In the book of Nehemiah, Sanballat and Tobiah were the enemies. They represent our spiritual enemy, the devil, whom we fight against even today. The devil tries to hinder our progress by throwing many roadblocks and troubles our way. He wants to stop us from making any progress in rebuilding the walls, closing gaps, or hanging gates.

"Now it happened, when Sanballat, Tobiah, the Arabs, the Ammonites, and the Ashdodites heard that the walls of Jerusalem were being restored and the gaps were beginning to be closed, that they became very angry, and all of them conspired together to come and attack Jerusalem and create confusion. Nevertheless we made our prayer to our God, and because of them we set a watch against them day and night" Nehemiah 4:7-9.

As they diligently worked on rebuilding the walls, the people displayed remarkable vigilance by not only employing tools for construction but also keeping a sword at their side.

"Those who built on the wall, and those who carried burdens, loaded themselves so that with one hand they worked at construction, and with the other held a weapon. Every one of the builders had his sword girded at his side as he built. And the one who sounded the trumpet was beside me" Nehemiah 4:17.

Their preparedness in both areas shows their understanding of the continuous danger posed by their opponents. While they focused on the physical task at hand, they remained armed and prepared to defend against any potential attacks. Every builder had his sword securely girded at his side, which represented his commitment to both the work of reconstruction and the defense against external challenges. The one sounding the trumpet stood beside Nehemiah, a testament to the coordinated effort and unified vigilance among the people.

As we strive to rebuild our emotional walls, the enemy will look to sow confusion and discord in our lives. As gaps begin to close, he gets angry. The New Testament talks about warfare, too. Paul talks about our putting on the armor of God.

"For we do not wrestle against flesh and blood, but against principalities, against powers, against the rulers of the darkness of this age, against spiritual hosts of wickedness in the heavenly places. Therefore take up the whole armor of God, that you may be able to withstand in the evil day, and having done all, to stand. Stand therefore, having girded your waist with truth, having put on the breastplate of righteousness, and having shod your feet with the preparation of the gospel of peace; above all, taking the shield of faith with which you will be able to quench all the fiery darts of the wicked one. And take the helmet of salvation, and the sword of the Spirit, which is the word of God; praying always with all prayer and supplication in the Spirit, being watchful to this end with all perseverance and supplication for all the saints" Ephesians 6:12-18.

We put on the armor of God to prepare ourselves to allow God to fight in our place. The Greek word used here for *put on* the armor is *enduo*. It has two primary meanings. The first is "to dress, to clothe someone," or "to clothe oneself in, to put on." Second, the word can be used figuratively and means to take on "characteristics, virtues, intentions."

We need to practice putting on the new man and walking in love, and the traits of Jesus will begin to become a part of our lives. If we follow Jesus and obey His Word, not just hear it, then the fruit of the Spirit will manifest in our lives. We will begin to show the characteristics of Jesus in how we conduct ourselves.

During our spiritual journey, we often face various battles, such as unforgiveness, doubt, fear, and addictions. These obstacles can prevent us from fully yielding to our heavenly Father. In times of spiritual warfare, it is crucial to acknowledge that God is in control and has our best interest in mind. We must trust that He knows the path ahead better than we do. Surrendering ourselves to God is essential, especially when we face difficulties, as it allows us to confront these obstacles effectively. This truth is beautifully echoed in the words spoken to Judah and Jerusalem:

"And he said, Listen, all you of Judah, and you inhabitants of Jerusalem, and you, King Jehoshaphat! Thus says the Lord to you, Do not be afraid nor dismayed because of this great multitude. For the battle is not yours, but God's" 2 Chronicles 20:15.

Similar reassurance is found in 1 Samuel, where we are reminded that victory does not come through conventional means:

"And all this assembly shall know that the Lord does not save with sword and spear; for the battle is Lord's, and He will give you into our hands" 1 Samuel 17:47.

Recognizing that the battle is the Lord's prompts a natural question: If we are not doing the fighting, how do we use this armor? Let's take a closer look at each piece of the spiritual armor and explore how we can effectively utilize each one in faith.

## THE BELT OF TRUTH

"Stand your ground, putting on the belt of truth" Ephesians 6:14 NLT.

The truth that we are to immerse ourselves in is God's truth. God's truth is the Bible. This truth keeps us secure in our faith in Christ and makes all the other armor pieces effective. The belt of truth holds all the different parts of our armor in place. To truly walk in the light of God's truth, commit to reading His Word daily:

"Sanctify them by Your truth. Your word is truth" John 17:17.

"Teach me your ways, O Lord; that I may live according to your truth!" Psalm 86:11 NLT

The belt of truth holds together our hearts and our minds.

**In the heart:** This kind of truth, in the heart, should influence our whole attitude. It should make us sincere and teachable before God. Holding malice and unforgiveness against someone will put a big dent in our armor.

**In our minds:** This means understanding sound doctrine. What do you believe? Are you aware of what Christ has done for you? Does the mental knowledge of Christ's victory on the cross translate into godly living in your life?

It will help strengthen our minds when we exert our wills over our flesh to serve the Lord. It is acting on what we know. A sincere heart and a determined mind together will give us a firm belt that keeps us rooted and grounded in Christ.

God's written Word is truth, and if you believe the written Word over our human reasoning or what circumstances may seem to indicate, then you are applying the Word of Truth. To put on this first piece of spiritual armor, we must immerse ourselves in Scripture. As we walk, sleep, and wake, we meditate on it:

"Keep their words always in your heart. Tie them around your neck. When you walk, their counsel will lead you. When you sleep, they will protect you" Proverbs 6:21-23 NLT.

Putting on the belt of truth, tying it tight, and meditating on it in our hearts is done by believing the Bible is the only truth. Things the world considers valid or our personal religious beliefs are not God's truth. It is essential to know what the Bible says and what it teaches. It is important to memorize passages and ask the Holy Spirit to guide you into all truth.

The truth of God's Word is not only our foundation but also our guide, just as Jesus exemplified when faced with temptation.

"Then Jesus was led up by the Spirit into the wilderness to be tempted by the devil. And when He had fasted forty days and forty nights, afterward He was hungry. Now when the tempter came to Him, he said, 'If You are the Son of God, command that these stones become bread.' But He answered and said, 'It is written, "Man shall not live by bread alone, but by every word that proceeds from the mouth of God."' Then the devil took Him up into the holy city, set Him on the pinnacle of the temple, and said to Him, "If You are the Son of God, throw Yourself down. For it is written: He shall give His angels charge over you, 'and, In their hands they shall bear you up, Lest you dash your foot against a stone.'" Jesus said to him, "It is written again, 'You shall not tempt the Lord your God.'" Again, the devil took Him up on an exceedingly high mountain and showed Him all the kingdoms of the world and their glory. And he said to Him, "All these things I will give You if You will fall down and worship me." Then Jesus said to him, "Away with you, Satan! For it is written, 'You shall worship the Lord your God, and Him only you shall serve.'" Then the devil left Him, and behold, angels came and ministered to Him" Matthew 4:1-11.

Putting on the belt is believing in the Word of God. We cannot depart from the authority of the Bible. Without the Bible as our foundation, we have no foundation at all. We must take all our authority from the Bible, or we have no authority. Biblical truth being demonstrated in our lives is when the Word and our actions become one. The Old Testament prophesied that the Messiah would come, and in the New Testament, Jesus came. The Word and the action became one. God's Word said the Messiah would come, and in due time, He did.

Our words and actions must align with our faith. Living no differently from the people in the world while claiming to have faith reveals a discrepancy from the truth. To truly live out the teachings of the Bible, we can't merely know them; we must actively practice them in our daily lives. It involves crucifying our flesh, putting Jesus on the throne, and embodying virtues like forgiveness without harboring desires for retribution. Whether it is forgiveness or any other virtue, we must not only be aware of it but also internalize and actively put it into practice. It requires us to stay committed to the truth and remain steadfast, even when it's difficult. As James rightly puts it: "But if you look carefully into the perfect law that sets you free, and if you do what it says and don't forget what you heard, then God will bless you for doing it" James 1:25.

## THE BREASTPLATE OF RIGHTEOUSNESS

"Stand therefore, having girded your waist with truth, having put on the breastplate of righteousness" Ephesians 6:14.

The breastplate protects the heart. The devil constantly attacks with lies, accusations, and reminders of past sins. Without the breastplate of righteousness, these will penetrate your heart. This is not our righteousness but Christ's. There is nothing we can do apart from Jesus, and He gives us His breastplate of righteousness to put on and wear.

It begins with justification through the blood of the cross and continues with new obedience of the believer. The principle of righteousness is implanted in the heart, a life governed according to the Word of God. As the breastplate protects the heart, lungs, and other vital organs, the righteousness of God covering our life defends everything on which a spiritual Christian life depends.

As the heart believes, our actions will follow. If you are not convinced you are righteous through Christ in God's eyes, if you have unbelief, anger, or disobedience, if you are tolerating sin or refusing to forgive, you have holes in the breastplate. Ask the Holy Spirit to show you where you are weakened in your armor. He will partner with you and help you work through any holes or blockages hindering your healing and wholeness.

## AND YOUR FEET SHOD WITH THE PREPARATION OF THE GOSPEL

"For shoes, put on the peace that comes from the Good News so that you will be fully prepared" Ephesians 6:15 NLT.

We need our feet shod with the steadfast and unwavering protection of faith and belief in Christ as our solid foundation. As we step out into life, we are called to walk a path filled with challenges and obstacles and engage in a race that demands perseverance and endurance. Our feet, firmly grounded on the rock of Christ's teachings and love, grant us the stability and strength needed for the challenges to our faith that lie ahead.

With each step we take, let us find peace in the knowledge that Christ's presence guides and sustains us, giving us the courage to face adversity head-on. Just as a pair of shoes protects our feet from injury, Christ's wisdom and grace shield us from the snares of doubt and despair.

Moreover, our path is not solely an individual walk but a collective pilgrimage with a community of believers. As we race forward, hand in hand, we uplift and support each other, fueled by the common bond of our faith in Christ. In times of doubt or weariness, we draw strength from the knowledge that we are not alone but part of a greater whole, and together, we can overcome any obstacle that hinders our progress.

As we march onward, our connection to Christ becomes the anchor that steadies us amid the storms of life. Like lamps along the way, His teachings light the path for our feet and give us clarity when the path seems unclear. We walk in His footsteps when we follow His example of compassion and kindness.

In times of celebration, we dance forward with hearts full of gratitude, acknowledging the blessings bestowed upon us. And in times of sorrow, we lean on Christ's ever-present love, finding solace in the assurance that He walks beside us, carrying us through the darkest valleys.

So let us continue this race with unwavering determination and the assurance that our feet are firmly anchored in the timeless truths of Christ's teachings. May our every step be a testament to our faith and devotion to our loving Savior, Jesus. In this endeavor, let's look at the wisdom of the apostle Paul:

"For no other foundation can anyone lay than that which is laid, which is Jesus Christ" 1 Corinthians 3:11.

As we press forward, let the unshakable foundation of Christ guide our every stride, ensuring that our race is run with purpose and endurance.

Our feet are prepared by being on our solid foundation of salvation in Jesus, knowing we have peace with God the Father through Him, and ready to go where He may lead. It means working to be at peace with others, not holding anger or blame against them, and living out the Word as an example to others that we are committed to Christ.

Commanded by God, the Israelites ate the Passover meal with sandals on their feet, representing that they were ready for their journey Exodus 12:11. Their sandals never wore out Deuteronomy 29:5. But in the end, they never entered the Promised Land because their feet slipped. They couldn't stay committed to God. They stopped short of what God had prepared for them.

We want to avoid making the same mistake. We don't want

our feet to slip. The deeper our relationship with the Father goes, the firmer our foundation in Christ will be. The deeper our feet are planted in the firm knowledge that we belong to the Father and He loves us, the more our faith will grow and the stronger our armor becomes.

## THE SHIELD OF FAITH

"Above all, taking the shield of faith with which you will be able to quench all the fiery darts of the wicked one" Ephesians 6:16.

The shield defends the whole body, protects the other pieces of our armor, and quenches all the fiery darts of the wicked one. Not just some—but all of them. The shield moves with the attack no matter which direction those fiery darts come from.

A shield will also deflect the enemy's weapons. Satan is always hurling fiery darts of fear, doubt, and worry in our direction. Our shield of faith protects us from harm, but it's only effective when we truly believe that God is in control and working everything out for our good. Even when things don't seem to be going our way, we must trust that everything is for the best of everyone involved. Only then can we truly be protected.

If you look at the different people mentioned in Hebrews 11, not all of them looked like a fabulous success from the world's point of view. In the latter part of the chapter, you will discover that some of them suffered cruel persecution. However, they never lost their confidence in the Lord whom they served. They were persuaded of the victory they had in God.

Taking up the shield of faith means we are trusting God is who He says He is and will protect us in the raging spiritual battle. Faith means that no matter what happens, we truly believe that God is there and will work things out for our good in His wisdom and understanding:

"Trust in the LORD with all your heart; and lean not on your own understanding. In all your ways, acknowledge him, and he shall direct your paths" Proverbs 3:5-6.

*Do I trust in God completely?* This serious question lies at the heart of our spiritual growth, asking us to examine the depth of our faith and reliance on our loving heavenly Father. From God alone comes our help, and His ever present Spirit living within us is a fact that extends far beyond our human understanding.

In our walk with God, we will encounter trials and challenges that seek to hinder us, but we find peace and strength in the refuge of God's loving arms. He holds the power to free us from the clutches of anything that might harbor ill intentions, guarding us from harm's way with a steadfast and watchful eye.

God's divine plan can be complex and difficult to understand, as it often unfolds in ways that extend beyond our limited understanding. In these moments of uncertainty, our faith faces its greatest test. Will we continue to trust Him, even when circumstances differ from our expectations or when our heartfelt prayers seem unanswered?

In moments of doubt, we must remind ourselves that God's wisdom extends far beyond our own understanding. God will always see things better than we do because He knows how everything will work out for the best, now and in our eternity with Him. To walk out our faith, we must place our complete confidence in Him and relinquish our tendency to rely on our limited human judgment.

The shield of faith serves as our divine armor, and its strength is derived from our trust in Him and an unwavering commitment to take God at His Word. We discover we have a spiritual defense in His divine wisdom, guidance, and promises that have stood steadfast throughout the ages, assuring us of God's unwavering love and compassion.

As we embrace the shield of faith, we acknowledge that God's plans may not always align with our desires, but He has our best interest in mind. Our walk of trust and faith is filled with rubble on our path. However, in the end, it is a dynamic and life-altering pilgrimage that shapes us into vessels useful to our Father God.

When we trust God implicitly, we go beyond the limitations of human understanding. In these precious moments, we draw closer to our God, discovering a connection with our Father through our Lord Jesus, which will go far beyond our earthly concerns.

So let us nurture our trust in God, for it's a beacon of light that guides us through life's dark passages. As we place our unwavering confidence in His infinite wisdom and embrace and hold high the shield of faith, we find ourselves walking amid the mysteries of His divine plan, knowing that in our surrender to His will, we uncover our true purpose and discover the unfathomable depth of His love and grace.

## THE HELMET OF SALVATION

"Put on salvation as your helmet" Ephesians 6:17 NLT.

The soldiers wore helmets to protect their heads. Similarly, our spiritual helmet of salvation protects our minds from the enemy's attempts to make us doubt God's Word, His promises, and our salvation. It safeguards our thoughts from questioning the truth behind the saving work of Jesus for us. It will guard our minds from the blows of the enemy.

A soldier could not fight with any strength in his heart if he thought there was no hope for victory. Likewise, a Christian can only contend with the enemy when there is the hope of final salvation, victory, and eternal life with the Father.

The fact that the helmet is compared to salvation shows that Satan's blows are directed at the believer's mind, attacking the hope of our security and assurance we have in Christ. He attacks our minds with discouragement, doubt, and fear. He points to our failures, sins, and emotional problems, scares us with poor health and financial insecurity, or whatever else seems negative in our lives to make us lose confidence and doubt in the love and care of our heavenly Father.

As believers, we draw strength from the promise of salvation, which serves as our protective helmet. This helmet symbolizes our unshakeable hope for ultimate salvation, assuring us that our struggle against Satan is only temporary and we will emerge victorious. We understand that this battle is limited to our time on earth, and even a long life here is nothing compared to the eternity we will spend with our Lord in heaven. We confidently approach this challenge, knowing we cannot lose this battle. As John 10 reminds us:

"And I give them eternal life, and they shall never perish; neither shall anyone snatch them out of My hand. 'My Father, who has given them to Me, is greater than all; and no one is able to snatch them out of My Father's hand'" John 10:28-29.

# THE SWORD OF THE SPIRIT

"And the sword of the Spirit, which is the word of God" Ephesians 6:17.

The sword in the armor serves not only as an offensive weapon but also as a tool for defense. The enemy uses strongholds, arguments, and thoughts as weapons against us, but with the sword of the Spirit, which is God's Word, we are empowered to face them all. Believing in the truth of God's Word and its value is critical. We must identify our personal scriptures in the Word to overcome our strongholds and use them as weapons. Therefore, it is vital to memorize the scriptures in order to wield this sword effectively.

To understand the nature of our spiritual battles, we turn to 2 Corinthians 10:

"For though we walk in the flesh, we do not war according to the flesh. For the weapons of our warfare are not carnal but mighty in God for pulling down strongholds, casting down arguments and every high thing that exalts itself against the knowledge of God, bringing every thought into captivity to the obedience of Christ, and being ready to punish all disobedience when your obedience is fulfilled" 2 Corinthians 10:3-6.

## FOR THE WEAPONS OF OUR WARFARE ARE NOT CARNAL

The tools we use in our battles are not physical weapons like those used by others in the world. We do not rely on superficial qualities like eloquence, talent, education, wealth, or beauty. Our strength comes from God, not from these external things.

## BUT MIGHTY THROUGH GOD

Our heavenly Father is the one who makes these weapons mighty and powerful. We have no hope for victory apart from our heavenly Father through His Son, Jesus.

## TO THE PULLING DOWN OF STRONGHOLDS

The term *strongholds* refers to fortresses and describes various obstacles that resemble fortresses. These obstacles are incorrect thinking patterns that exist in our minds and are programmed to think in opposition to the truth.

## CASTING DOWN IMAGINATIONS

What are the imaginations in this verse? It is anything contrary to the Word of God. Most imaginations are lies. We are to cast down (throw it out with great force) any opposing thoughts that arise in our minds. There's no need to waste time trying to reason with them.

## AND EVERY HIGH THING

Any human understanding or wisdom contrary to God's Word that we believe (exalt) over the Word of God is a "high thing." If it opposes God's knowledge, yet we refuse to let go of it, we elevate our understanding over God's. Our human wisdom and knowledge can lead to pride.

## AND BRINGING INTO CAPTIVITY

We must demolish the strongholds of sin, pride, fear, unforgiveness, and anything exalting itself over God's Word. As we do, our minds come under Christ's authority (captivity). All our thoughts and plans must come under the control of the will of God and not our own. We need to allow the Father to take us captive and let Him plan our lives. We must be serious about our faith, hiding it in our hearts (Psalm 119:11).

## PRAYER

"Pray in the Spirit at all times and on every occasion. Stay alert and be persistent in your prayers for all believers everywhere" Ephesians 6:18 NLT.

Remember this crucial piece of armor! Prayer is the most important! Our armor will only be complete with prayer. If our prayer life is strong, we will not be defeated. God alone can give the victory, and when the Christian goes forth completely armed for the spiritual conflict, if we look to God in faith and prayer, we can be sure He has heard us. We are not to pray occasionally; it is to be always.

Let us anchor ourselves in unwavering reliance on prayer and listen to the wisdom of Nehemiah, who encouraged us not to be afraid. Nehemiah, facing challenges, rallied the people, saying:

"Then as I looked over the situation, I called together the nobles and the rest of the people and said to them, 'Don't be afraid of the enemy! Remember the Lord, who is great and glorious, and fight for your brothers, your sons, your daughters, your wives, and your homes!'" Nehemiah 4:14 NLT

During difficult times, it's important to focus on God for strength and courage. We should stand up for what is important in our lives, relying on prayer and being determined, knowing that God will empower us to face any challenge. As we confront the spiritual challenges before us, let us also heed the lesson from Psalm 78:9, which warns about the enemy's subtle plan to keep us spiritually unproductive: "The children of Ephraim, being armed, and carrying bows, turned back in the day of battle" Psalm 78:9.

The people who possessed the weapons decided not to use them and turned back instead. Do we sometimes turn back or refuse to go forward? If we know what the Word says but only hear it and do not practice it, we are turning back in the day of battle.

In order to fulfill our responsibility to learn and embody the Scriptures, we can take guidance from Philippians as it serves as a guide, encouraging us to live out the Word:

"The things which you learned and received and heard and saw in me, these do, and the God of peace will be with you" Philippians 4:9.

In the book of Daniel, Shadrach, Meshach, and Abednego, confronted with the threat of a fiery furnace, declared their unwavering faith:

"Our God whom we serve is able to deliver us from the burning fiery furnace, and he will deliver us from your hand, O king. But if not, be it known to you, O king, that we do not serve your gods, nor will we worship the image which you have set up" Daniel 3:17-18.

These verses emphasize the significance of having unwavering faith in God despite our circumstances. Therefore, as we dig into God's Word, let us not only gain knowledge but also develop a deep, life-changing faith. May the truths of Scripture become so deeply rooted in our hearts that we can confidently declare, like Shadrach, Meshach, and Abednego, "He can rescue me, but even if He doesn't, I still wholly trust in Him."

Through this crucial integration of faith and action, we can build an unshakable foundation for facing any trial, knowing that the God of peace is with us.

As we strengthen our faith by aligning our actions with the Word of God, we build a strong foundation that empowers us to face any challenge with the assurance that the God of peace is with us. In times of fear, we can draw strength from Second Timothy:

"For God has not given us a spirit of fear, but of power and of love and of a sound mind" 2 Timothy 1:7.

Fear may grip us, but we do not want to act out of fear. Fear must not restrain us from upholding the Word of God in our hearts and actions. Anxiety will decrease with time, practice, and patience, and our faith in God will strengthen. When bad news comes, we need strength from the Lord. It does not mean we stuff our feelings or emotions. We can express ourselves and our tears to our heavenly Father because He understands.

In the end, however, we want to trust in the will of God in whatever He has for us, even if we disagree with Him, even if things look bad, trusting in Him no matter what the future holds. Now that's faith.

Loving Heavenly Father,

I pray for the strength to put on the full armor of God. Equip me to battle against fear, addiction, and anything that hinders my relationship with You. I acknowledge that You are in control, and I trust in Your wisdom even when I do not understand. Help me to surrender completely to Your plan, knowing that You always work for my best.

Lord, deepen my faith so that I can stand strong against the enemy by believing in Your promises. Show me where my words and actions do not align with Your Word, and grant me the courage to make necessary changes.

In moments of doubt, help me to remain faithful and not rely on myself. Remind me that I have victory through Christ, regardless of how things appear. I commit to bringing every thought captive to Your truth.

In Jesus' name, I pray, amen.

# CHAPTER 10
# THE EAST GATE

*"After him Shemaiah the son of Shechaniah, the keeper of the East Gate, made repairs."*
Nehemiah 3:29

The East Gate was probably named so because it faced the east direction. It's worth noting that the East Gate mentioned during the rebuilding of Jerusalem's wall in the fifth century BCE by Nehemiah is not the same as the one present today. Throughout history, the wall has been destroyed by enemies and rebuilt again.

According to Jewish tradition, the Messiah would enter Jerusalem through this gate. Interestingly, during the sixteenth century, Sultan Suleiman the Magnificent, a Turkish ruler, ordered the entrance of the East Gate to be blocked with huge stones. It is believed he did this to prevent the Messiah from coming.

The East Gate has been blocked for centuries and remains blocked to this day, and it stands as a testament to the deliberate actions taken in the past to obstruct the Messiah. This serves as a powerful reminder to us to keep our hearts unobstructed and eagerly await the fulfillment of God's promises. It encourages us to live with hope for Jesus' return. In Matthew, Jesus vividly describes His second coming, saying that it will be like lightning that flashes from the east to the west.

"For as the lightning comes from the east and flashes to the west, so also will the coming of the Son of Man be" Matthew 24:7.

As believers, we are called to pray for and eagerly anticipate Jesus' coming, all the while abiding in Him and seeking His guidance and wisdom:

"But [we are different, because] our citizenship is in heaven. And from there we eagerly await [the coming of] the Savior, the Lord Jesus Christ; who, by exerting that power which enables Him even to subject everything to Himself, will [not only] transform [but completely refashion] our earthly bodies so that they will be like His glorious resurrected body" Philippians 3:20 AMP.

"Your kingdom come, Your will be done, on earth as it is in heaven" Matthew 6:10.

"He who is the faithful witness to all these things says, 'Yes, I am coming soon!'

Amen! Come, Lord Jesus!" Revelation 22:20.

Thanks to Jesus, when He returns, we can confidently approach God's presence without fear of shame or inadequacy:

"And now, dear children, remain in fellowship with Christ so that when he returns, you will be full of courage and not shrink back from him in shame" 1 John 2:28 NLT.

There is also a crown of righteousness for all believers who eagerly await His return:

"Finally, there is laid up for me the crown of righteousness, which the Lord, the righteous Judge, will give to me on that Day, and not to me only but also to all who have loved His appearing" 2 Timothy 4:8.

How do we await Christ's return while ensuring our hearts

remain prepared? Let's look at this verse from Nehemiah that mentions gatekeepers:

"Moreover the gatekeepers, Akkub, Talmon, and their brethren who kept the gates, were one hundred and seventy-two" Nehemiah 11:19.

Over time, as we strive to grow spiritually, sin will still raise its ugly head, our walls will get weak, and our gates will get creaky. While we wait for Christ's return, we must be the keeper of our gates.

"And I said to them, 'Do not let the gates of Jerusalem be opened until the sun is hot; and while they stand guard, let them shut and bar the doors; and appoint guards from among the inhabitants of Jerusalem, one at his watch station and another in front of his own house'" Nehemiah 7:3.

Even after Nehemiah constructed the wall, he understood how important continued vigilance was. The presence of gatekeepers and guards signifies an ongoing commitment to the protection of that wall.

As we embark on our spiritual path, it is essential to recognize that the presence of sin in our lives is an ongoing reality. No matter how much progress we make, sin tends to resurface, reminding us of our imperfections and challenging our commitment to spiritual development.

The wall and gates of Nehemiah can help illustrate this concept. In spiritual growth, our walls represent the boundaries and defenses we establish using the Word of God to guard our hearts and minds against negative influences and sinful behaviors.

However, over time, our walls can develop gaps and holes. This imagery reflects the vulnerabilities and weaknesses that can appear within us. We may become complacent, allowing certain negative habits or thoughts to seep through the cracks in our defenses. These imperfections remind us that we are not immune to temptation and that spiritual maturity requires constant vigilance.

In the same way, our gates symbolize the entry points to our inner selves—our thoughts, desires, and intentions. As keepers of our gates, we must be mindful of what we allow to enter our souls. We must exercise discernment, carefully filtering the influences that seek to shape our character. Neglecting our role as gatekeepers can result in the infiltration of harmful consequences that hinder our spiritual growth.

In addition to being gatekeepers, we also need to be watchers on the wall of our souls. "Keep watch and pray, so that you will not give in to temptation. For the spirit is willing, but the body is weak" Mark 14:38.

This role involves being alert and vigilant. By paying close attention to our thoughts, emotions, and behaviors, we understand where we need to improve and identify potential sources of sin. The watcher on the wall actively seeks to maintain the integrity of his or her spiritual life and takes proactive steps to address any vulnerabilities.

It is important to understand that recognizing sin and the fact that we are imperfect does not diminish the significance of our spiritual growth. Instead, it serves as a reminder of our humanity and the ongoing need for humility, self-reflection, and total reliance on our Lord Jesus. Through persistence and a genuine desire for change, we can strengthen our walls and repair our gates by deepening our spiritual relationship with God. This is our goal and will give us value and purpose.

As followers of Christ, it is crucial to listen carefully to the teachings of the Bible and apply them in our everyday lives. The Bible emphasizes the significance of obedience and the life-changing impact of God's Word when it is taken to heart and acted upon with faith. Protecting our minds and guarding our thoughts is crucial to keeping a healthy spiritual walk with our heavenly Father.

Philippians 4:8 encourages believers to dwell on true, noble, just, pure, lovely, commendable, excellent, and praiseworthy things. Focusing on these aspects can prevent negative or impure thoughts from taking root in our minds.

It's important to recognize that we all have weaknesses and may occasionally falter in our faith. Our defenses may weaken, and our hearts can become blocked again, making us vulnerable to negative influences. However, this is a normal part of spiritual growth and emphasizes our ongoing need for God's grace and guidance.

When we find ourselves in such a state, we must turn to God in repentance and seek His forgiveness and restoration. First John 1:9 assures us that if we confess our sins, God is faithful and just to forgive us and cleanse us from all unrighteousness. We can renew our minds and restore our spiritual vitality by praying, asking for guidance from the Holy Spirit, and immersing ourselves in God's Word. Being a doer of His Word is how we become a watchman on the wall.

It's important to remember that our faith journey is not always straightforward, and setbacks are not indications of failure. The stones of our walls may get burned and black again, but they can remind us of our continual need for reliance on God's strength and grace. As we persevere, seek God's help, and surround ourselves with supportive fellow believers, we can find the strength to overcome obstacles and continue growing in our faith.

Growing in faith is a race we must run until we go to Jesus or He returns to earth.

"Don't you realize that in a race everyone runs, but only one person gets the prize? So run to win! All athletes are disciplined in their training. They do it to win a prize that will fade away, but we do it for an eternal prize. So I run with purpose in every step. I am not just shadowboxing. I discipline my body like an athlete, training it to do what it should. Otherwise, I fear that after preaching to others I myself might be disqualified" 1 Corinthians 9:24-27 NLT.

But as we run our race, what happens when we falter, and the stones in our walls get burned once again? Can we really revive them again? The enemy will lie and tell us we can't, just as he scoffed at the Jews in Nehemiah's time, calling them feeble:

"And he spoke before his brethren and the army of Samaria, and said, 'What are these feeble Jews doing? Will they fortify themselves? Will they offer sacrifices? Will they complete it in a day? Will they revive the stones from the heaps of rubbish—stones that are burned?' " Nehemiah 4:2.

But indeed, we can! It is possible to revive the stones time and time again through the divine intervention of Jesus. When we falter, it's a critical moment that demands reflection and a renewed reliance on God's strength. The key to accomplishing this is to open ourselves up to Him and allow Him to break through our east gate that might once again be cluttered with debris and obstruct our path. With faith and trust in Him, we can be confident that He will restore us with His mighty resurrection power that now also lives in us.

"I also pray that you will understand the incredible greatness of God's power for us who believe him. This is the same mighty power that raised Christ from the dead and seated him in the place of honor at God's right hand in the heavenly realms" Ephesians 1:19-20.

"But if the Spirit of Him who raised Jesus from the dead dwells in you, He who raised Christ from the dead will also give life to your mortal bodies through His Spirit who dwells in you" Romans 8:11-12.

As believers, we must remain steadfast in our faith and keep our eyes fixed on Jesus, striving to live a life that honors Him and fulfills His will for our lives. We must persevere through the challenges and obstacles we might face, knowing that our goal is to be with Him in eternity. Whether He returns to earth in our lifetimes or not, we must continue to run this race with endurance, trusting in His grace and strength to carry us through.

The story of Nehemiah provides a powerful example of the importance of maintaining unwavering faith, especially in the face of challenges. Only a select few chose to travel to Jerusalem despite the possibility of facing adversity:

"Now the leaders of the people dwelt at Jerusalem; the rest of the people cast lots to bring one out of ten to dwell in Jerusalem, the holy city, and nine-tenths were to dwell in other cities. And the people blessed all the men who willingly offered themselves to dwell at Jerusalem" Nehemiah 11:1-2.

After being exiled, many people chose not to return to Jerusalem and instead preferred to stay where they were comfortable. According to the Scripture, while the leaders lived in Jerusalem, only one out of every ten people followed them. Leaving the place of exile was not an easy decision, as staying there felt more secure than going to Jerusalem, where they could face severe difficulties. Those who decided to leave would have to start their lives all over again. It would cost them a lot to make such a move.

In the New Testament, we also come across the commitment to endurance:

"Now great multitudes went with Him. And He turned and said to them, "If anyone comes to Me and does not hate his father and mother, wife and children, brothers and sisters, yes, and his own life also, he cannot be My disciple. And whoever does not bear his cross and come after Me cannot be My disciple. For which of you, intending to build a tower, does not sit down first and count the cost, whether he has enough to finish it— lest, after he has laid the foundation, and is not able to finish, all who see it begin to mock him, saying, 'This man began to build and was not able to finish'? Or what king, going to make war against another king, does not sit down first and consider whether he is able with ten thousand to meet him who comes against him with twenty thousand? Or else, while the other is still a great way off, he sends a delegation and asks conditions of peace. So likewise, whoever of you does not forsake all that he has cannot be My disciple" Luke 14:25-33.

The call to follow Jesus is accompanied by a weighty challenge. It echoes the words of Jesus in Luke 14, where He emphasizes the significant cost of discipleship. The crowds that followed Him were numerous, but Jesus made it clear that true discipleship demands more than mere attendance. He presented the analogy of building a tower or going to war, emphasizing the need to count the cost before making a commitment. Just as those who considered returning to Jerusalem had to weigh the sacrifices, Jesus invites us to ponder the cost of following Him.

It will cost you to enter the kingdom of God. The commitment required is deep and life-changing. The call to forsake all, to prioritize God's kingdom over even the closest relationships and one's own life, mirrors the difficult choice faced by the exiled people. This choice is not to be taken lightly, as Jesus warns against starting the task without considering the full implications.

So as you reflect on the exiles' struggle and Jesus' teachings, consider the parallels in your own life. Will you surrender your life to our heavenly Father? Are you willing to follow Jesus, no matter the cost? Just as the exiles had to weigh the challenges of returning to Jerusalem against the comfort of staying, we, too, must carefully consider the demands of true discipleship. The decision to follow Jesus may require leaving behind familiar comforts, starting anew, and embracing a life-changing process that comes at a significant cost but leads to the richness of life in the kingdom of God.

Powerful Heavenly Father,

I lift my gaze in anticipation of Christ's return. I pray for the strength to clear the path in my life for the King of Kings, removing any obstacles that hinder His presence. Grant me continued vigilance as a gatekeeper and watcher on the wall in my life. May I stand in unwavering faith, eagerly awaiting the glorious return of my Savior.

Lord, help me persist in the ongoing work on weak or sinful areas in my life. Grant me the courage to confront and overcome, knowing Your grace empowers transformation. In moments of setbacks, may I not be deterred from the race set before me. Strengthen my resolve to persevere, counting the cost of following Jesus with joy and dedication.

In Jesus' name, I pray, amen.

## CHAPTER 11
# THE INSPECTION GATE

> "After him Malchijah, one of the goldsmiths, made repairs as far as the house of the Nethinim and of the merchants, in front of the Miphkad Gate, and as far as the upper room at the corner."
> Nehemiah 3:31

According to tradition, the Miphkad (mif-kawd) or inspection gate was the gate where David met his troops for inspection. This gate, associated with the accountability of soldiers and their deeds, serves as a reminder of the ultimate inspection we will all face. The Inspection Gate reminds us of the bema seat of Christ, where our lives will be thoroughly examined and justly rewarded. Those who have been faithful will receive their due rewards. We should focus on the eternal rather than the temporary things we encounter daily.

As the apostle Paul writes in 2 Corinthians:

"Therefore we make it our aim, whether present or absent, to be well pleasing to Him. For we must all appear before the judgment seat of Christ, that each one may receive the things done in the body, according to what he has done, whether good or bad" 2 Corinthians 5:9-10.

How can we hold up to a final inspection by the Father God?

Only by the blood of Jesus. Salvation through Christ is what makes us holy. When we are genuinely saved, we will want to please the Father and obey His Word. We must also inspect our lives each day and repent when we fall short. We need to take a close look at our thoughts and actions. Do they line up with God's Word?

Did we live for ourselves or God? The King will return, and the servants will give an account Luke 19:11-26. Did we put our hands to the plow or look back Luke 9:62? Were our words to others gracious? We want to stand before Jesus with joy and confidence, so we must build our walls (lives) with precious stones and gold and silver 1 Corinthians 3:10-15. Our ultimate goal is to lay up treasures in heaven, where neither decay nor theft can diminish their eternal worth.

"Don't store up treasures here on earth, where moths eat them and rust destroys them, and where thieves break in and steal. Store your treasures in heaven, where moths and rust cannot destroy, and thieves do not break in and steal. Wherever your treasure is, there the desires of your heart will also be" Matthew 6:19-21 NLT.

As we make our way through the gates, our paths lead us back to the Sheep Gate.

"After him Malchijah, one of the goldsmiths, made repairs as far as the house of the Nethinim and of the merchants, in front of the Miphkad Gate, and as far as the upper room at the corner. And between the upper room at the corner, as far as the Sheep Gate, the goldsmiths and the merchants made repairs" Nehemiah 3:31-32.

Everything begins and ends with Christ. The Sheep Gate is where Christ saved us, and we will eventually stand before Him at the Inspection Gate. Christ is the beginning and end of all things. He is the Alpha and the Omega Revelation 1:8. From beginning with Christ through salvation to being united with Him forever, we are victorious, and the enemy will resent it. And the devil knows full well that our God was with us every step of the way:

"When our enemies and the surrounding nations heard about it, they were frightened and humiliated. They realized this work had been done with the help of our God" Nehemiah 6:16 NLT.

Rebuilding your emotional wall will make the devil unhappy because he wants to keep you fragmented and emotionally crippled. Remember, he can only try to make you believe his lies. Your progress toward wholeness is essential; he will always try to prevent it. So we must be on our guard. After Nehemiah left, the enemy and old thinking began to set in once again:

"Before this had happened, Eliashib the priest, who had been appointed as supervisor of the storerooms of the Temple of our God and who was also a relative of Tobiah, had converted a large storage room and placed it at Tobiah's disposal. The room had previously been used for storing the grain offerings, the frankincense, various articles for the Temple, and the tithes of grain, new wine, and olive oil (which were prescribed for the Levites, the singers, and the gatekeepers), as well as the offerings for the priests. I was not in Jerusalem at that time, for I had returned to King Artaxerxes of Babylon in the thirty-second year of his reign, though I later asked his permission to return. When I arrived back in Jerusalem, I learned about Eliashib's evil deed in providing Tobiah with a room in the courtyards of the Temple of God. I became very upset and threw all of Tobiah's belongings out of the room. Then I demanded that the rooms be purified, and I brought back the articles for God's Temple, the grain offerings, and the frankincense" Nehemiah 13:4-9 NLT.

Nehemiah completed the work and returned to the king. In his absence, Eliashib, the priest, gave Tobiah one of the inner chamber rooms in the temple. Now Tobiah was the enemy! Tobiah had tried his best to stop the rebuilding of the wall, and yet the priest still cleaned out a room for him. Notice that the Scripture says Eliashib had authority over the rooms. Tobiah filled the room that formally held holy things with his possessions. When Nehemiah returned and discovered the chamber defiled, he was grieved and threw it all out; he then had the room cleansed and the holy items returned.

"I also discovered that the Levites had not been given their prescribed portions of food, so they and the singers who were to conduct the worship services had all returned to work their fields. I immediately confronted the leaders and demanded, 'Why has the Temple of God been neglected?' Then I called all the Levites back again and restored them to their proper duties" Nehemiah 13:10-11 NLT.

As Nehemiah addressed external challenges and had the defiled chamber cleaned, he turned his attention inward. The Levites, responsible for worship and other duties, had not been receiving their prescribed food portions and were forced to return to work in the fields, leaving them unable to serve the Lord. Discovering this neglect, Nehemiah confronted the leaders, demanding, 'Why has the temple of God been neglected?' He promptly called the Levites back and restored them to their duties.

Our minds and souls are our "temples," where we also have hidden chambers. We must be careful not to neglect God's Word and pay attention to what we store in our minds. Just like Eliashib had authority over the rooms, we have authority over our minds. If we are not watchful, we can give place to the enemy and allow things to enter that will defile our minds through unforgiveness, addictions, thoughts, and even the words we speak about ourselves and others.

The common pattern is to clean out these chambers momentarily with good intentions. However, over time, old ways and thinking creep back in, occupying the sacred space meant for God's holiness. Our focus should be on continuous spiritual growth, resisting the pullback to former habits. Repentance and restoration to our "proper duties" of following Jesus are essential when we find ourselves veering off course.

When we neglect our spiritual growth, things in our chambers again get dusty. We need to take an inventory of ourselves periodically. Are we further along than we were a few months ago? We all fall short at some point and need to get back on track. Throughout our lives, we must check for holes in the walls and plug them up again. Rebuilding the wall will be an ongoing process. We must work out our salvation with fear and trembling:

"Dear friends, you always followed my instructions when I was with you. And now that I am away, it is even more important. Work hard to show the results of your salvation, obeying God with deep reverence and fear" Philippians 2:12 NLT.

Once the wall and gates are in place, we must rule our minds and constantly make faith choices, or the wall will be in ruin again. This echoes the apostle Paul's call to the Philippians, emphasizing the importance of working hard to manifest the results of our salvation. It requires ongoing effort to obey God with deep reverence and fear. Just as a city without walls is vulnerable, so too is a mind without discipline. We must practice self-discipline in our actions, thoughts, and feelings.

As this verse in Proverbs wisely asserts: "Whoever has no

rule over his own spirit is like a city broken down, without walls" Proverbs 25:28.

The word translated as *rule* in Hebrew is *matsar*, which means temperance or self-control. It's restraint exercised over our impulses, emotions, or desires.

To rule over our minds means to actively engage in the process of making faith choices. Faith choices encompass decisions that align with the Word of God. They require us to cultivate deep discernment, constantly evaluating our thoughts, intentions, and motivations. By consciously choosing faith over doubt, hope over despair, and love over fear, we reinforce the foundations of our healthy walls.

Once the wall and gates are in place, representing the healthier boundaries and defenses we establish to protect ourselves and our relationship with our heavenly Father, we embark on a path of self-discipline. It is not enough to construct these walls; we must also take responsibility for governing our minds and exercising conscious control over our thoughts, actions, and emotions. This is essential to ensure that the rebuilt Nehemiah wall remain sturdy and impenetrable.

Self-discipline is not just limited to controlling our thoughts, but it also involves our actions, behavior towards others, and the way we express our emotions. To practice self-discipline, we need to align our actions with God's Word and make consistent efforts to do so. It requires us to resist the temptation of instant gratification, which may harm our long-term goals and our relationship with God. The apostle Paul, in one of his letters, stressed the importance of self-discipline and its impact on our lives:

"But I discipline my body and bring it into subjection: lest, when I have preached to others, I myself should be disqualified" 1 Corinthians 9:27.

The path of self-discipline and ruling over our minds is a challenging one. It demands dedication, perseverance, and the willingness to confront our weaknesses and limitations. It may involve letting go of addictions and unhealthy habits, questioning deeply ingrained biases, or challenging negative thought patterns. It is a continual process of growth, self-reflection, learning, and putting God's Word into practice. It is a daily practice of learning to hear the Holy Spirit.

Please don't feel discouraged; this process will continue throughout your lifetime here on earth. The process of spiritual growth is a lifelong commitment, and just as Nehemiah diligently worked to rebuild the wall of Jerusalem, we, too, must remain steadfast in the ongoing process of fortifying our spiritual wall.

It's important to remember that this is ongoing and has no time limit. We are constantly faced with new challenges, temptations, and opportunities for growth. Through dedication to discipline, we reinforce the healthy walls we are rebuilding and protect the gates of our minds, eyes, and ears. When we do have moments of discouragement, it is crucial to remind ourselves of the ever-present power of God and how He can use our self-discipline. Each choice we make, every act of conscious alignment with God's Word, strengthens our resilience and fortifies the walls we have built. Though setbacks and failures may occur, they in no way mean defeat. Instead, they serve as opportunities for learning, refinement, and renewed commitment to the journey.

By ruling over our minds and practicing discipline, we become active participants in our spiritual and personal growth, forming a partnership with the Father, Jesus, and the Holy Spirit. As we travel through life with the ongoing process of ruling over our minds, it enables us to create a life of purpose, integrity, and fulfillment through our Lord Jesus.

Overcoming addiction or emotional disorders requires self-control. It's essential to acknowledge the empowering message of the Word and believe in our ability to exercise self-control. This becomes the foundation for change. Declare to yourself that you can take control of your thoughts, willpower, emotions, and physical senses and submit them to the life-changing power of God's Word.

The passage in 2 Peter aligns with biblical teaching and encourages believers to practice self-control as a part of their spiritual growth. It urges us to diligently cultivate different virtues in addition to our faith, with self-control being an essential and crucial one:

"But also for this very reason, giving all diligence, add to your faith virtue, to virtue knowledge, to knowledge self-control, to self-control, perseverance, to perseverance godliness, to godliness brotherly kindness, and to brotherly kindness love" 2 Peter 1:5-6.

It is essential to have self-control and rule over your mind. Once saved through Christ, we have new hearts where God provides us with beautiful qualities within our souls to help us be obedient to His Word. It is our choice. We have free will to choose God's way or not.

The apostle Paul lists temperance (self-control) as an attribute of your recreated human spirit:

"But the fruit of the spirit is love, joy, peace, long suffering, gentleness, goodness, faith, Meekness, temperance: against such there is no law" Galatians 5:22-23.

As a believer, it is crucial to understand that we have the ability, through Christ, to control our desires and rule over our spirits. With the guidance of the Word of God and the power of the Holy Spirit, He can empower our spirits to gain mastery over our minds, bodies, and emotions. Discipline may be challenging. There is a price to pay when we choose obedience. Denying oneself and choosing the cross is work. Rebuilding the fallen walls is work. Some choose not to do the work. Some of us get weary from the work. God is faithful and will be there as you persevere in your spiritual growth. Remember, it is not how we feel or what we see; it is believing in God's promises. And He promises to restore us if we will seek Him: "You, who have shown me great and severe troubles, shall revive me again; and bring me up again from the depths of the earth" Psalm 71:20.

To live according to the Scriptures, we must study and apply them to our lives:

"For if you live according to the flesh you will die; but if by the Spirit you put to death the deeds of the body, you will live" Romans 8:13.

While the path of discipline may be challenging, choosing obedience and denying oneself is the necessary work of rebuilding fallen walls. Some may find the labor daunting, and weariness may set in, yet God remains faithful and promises restoration to those who persevere in their spiritual growth. The book of Revelation tells us:

"And he who overcomes, and keeps My works until the end, to him I will give power over the nations" Revelation 2:26.

For followers of Christ, salvation marks only the beginning of an incredible experience. True believers must strive to live a life that represents the teachings of Jesus to become "overcomers." Becoming an overcomer is a challenging feat and requires diligent effort and action. The New Testament mentions the word *overcometh* eleven times, emphasizing the importance of this designation for believers. It is not enough to simply accept Christ as one's Savior—one must also actively seek to obey God's Word and keep His commandments to become an overcomer. Let us strive to become true overcomers and inherit the amazing rewards that come with it.

"Everyone who believes that Jesus is the Christ has become a child of God. And everyone who loves the Father loves his children, too. We know we love God's children if we love God and obey his commandments. Loving God means keeping his commandments, and his commandments are not burdensome. For every child of God defeats this evil world, and we achieve this victory through our faith" 1 John 5:1-5 NLT.

As believers, we should always strive to maintain our faith and deepen our relationship with the Father. If we remain diligent in running our race, we can be assured we will not experience fear or shame when facing our Lord Jesus. So we must be intentional in our efforts to grow spiritually, seek wisdom and understanding through His Word, pray, read and study the Word, and live a life pleasing to Him. We must also be willing to rely on the Holy Spirit to guide, convict, and empower us to live the life God has called us to live. Our ultimate aim should be to hear the Father's words of commendation:

"And he said to him, 'Well done, good servant, because you have been faithful in a least thing, have authority over ten cities' " Luke 19:17.

May we always keep our eyes fixed on Jesus, the author and

finisher of our faith, and may we never lose sight of the goal of hearing those words, "Well done, good and faithful servant."

Dear Heavenly Father,

I humbly ask for Your guidance and insight. Help me identify areas where I fall short; grant me the courage to see my shortcomings through Your eyes. Teach me that rebuilding walls takes time and patience. In this process, I ask You to cleanse any hidden "rooms" in my mind where I have allowed the enemy to dwell. May I be vigilant and intentional in maintaining the integrity of my thoughts.

Lord, I acknowledge that rebuilding is a daily ongoing process. Help me to rule my mind and instill in me the discipline of self-control, especially in areas of weakness. I thank You for Your help in rebuilding my healthier "Nehemiah" wall. I will cast out moments of discouragement and replace it with Your unwavering hope.

Father, I desire to be an overcomer by keeping Your Word and living it out. Knowing I won't be perfect, I come before You with humility and repentance when I fail. Keep my eyes fixed on Jesus, the author, and finisher of my faith.

In His name, I pray, amen.

# CHAPTER 12
# SO I'M RESTORED NOW, RIGHT?

"So the wall was finished on the twenty-fifth day of Elul, in fifty-two days. And it happened, when all our enemies heard of it, and all the nations around us saw these things, that they were very disheartened in their own eyes; for they perceived that this work was done by our God."
Nehemiah 6:15-16

The Scripture says the wall was built in just fifty-two days, displaying remarkable speed and efficiency in erecting the physical structure. However, it is important to recognize the significance of the wall extends beyond their construction and rapid completion. The true importance lies in the ongoing maintenance and fortification of the wall.

Walls serve as a protective barrier, shielding what is inside from external threats and dangers. Physical walls can be attacked, damaged, and require repair. In the same way, our emotional and spiritual boundaries can face similar challenges. The cracks, gaps, and hidden chambers within our hearts and minds must not be neglected, as these will be the very vulnerabilities that our adversary takes advantage of.

In parallel to maintaining physical walls, we must pay attention to the areas within ourselves that may have been wounded or weakened by past hurts and offenses. One of the most challenging tasks is forgiving those who have wronged us. It encompasses forgiving not only past transgressions but also present and future ones.

However, it is essential for our well-being that we learn this valuable lesson. By forgiving others, we free ourselves from the weight of demanding justice for the wrong done to us. This liberating act allows us to move forward, unburdened by the unforgiveness that can poison our hearts and hinder our growth. When we choose forgiveness, we open the door to healing, restoration, and personal transformation.

When we accepted Christ into our lives, He began a work of changing our hearts. By surrendering to His will in all aspects of our lives, we allow Him to complete that work. Through this surrender and dependence on Him, we find the strength and perseverance to forgive, even in the most challenging circumstances.

Moreover, as believers, we have victory through Jesus. His sacrifice and resurrection have granted us access to His Word and the guidance of the Holy Spirit. We are not alone in our pursuit of forgiveness and spiritual growth. The saints in the Bible serve as examples, cheering us on as we face life's challenges.

The lesson of the wall goes beyond their construction in a mere fifty-two days. It is about maintaining and fortifying our emotional and spiritual boundaries. We must understand that forgiveness is crucial in this process, freeing us from the burdens of wanting restitution. By relying on Jesus, His Word, and the Holy Spirit's guidance, we can endure the journey of forgiveness, knowing we have the assurance that Christ will bring His work in us to completion (Philippians 1:6). The Word also calls us living stones, with Christ serving as our unshakable Cornerstone:

"You are coming to Christ, who is the living cornerstone of God's temple. He was rejected by people, but he was chosen by God for great honor. And you are living stones that God is building into his spiritual temple. What's more, you are his holy priests. Through the mediation of Jesus Christ, you offer spiritual sacrifices that please God. As the Scriptures say, "I am placing a cornerstone in Jerusalem, chosen for great honor, and anyone who trusts in him will never be disgraced" 1 Peter 2:4-6 NLT.

At first glance, a stone might not seem incredibly functional or pretty. However, a skilled landscaper can convert it into a work of art, transforming it into an integral part of a beautiful and serviceable space. Stones have been used for centuries to construct sturdy foundations due to their strength and durability. In the same way, when we build our lives on the foundation of the Chief Cornerstone Jesus, He can mold us into something valuable, beautiful, and useful in the hands of our Creator God.

In our modern society, there is an increasing demand for instant gratification, which seems especially true when it comes to personal healing, addiction recovery, and emotional well-being. It's only natural for us to want to feel better right away, and if we don't see the results we're hoping for, it's easy to become discouraged or even resentful towards our heavenly Father. Sometimes we might even feel compelled to take matters into our own hands or abandon our faith altogether. It's important to keep in mind that genuine healing requires time. We must have faith in the process and be patient as we face life's numerous challenges.

Maintaining a focus on our heavenly Father requires discipline in our everyday lives. We must be patient and trust in His timing and how He works rather than in ourselves. It takes faith to believe He is working things out for us, even when we can't feel it, or it looks like nothing is changing. The path of our spiritual race is far from easy. Many Bible saints in the Old and New Testaments had extremely tough lives. Yet they kept their faith in the almighty God, even when it meant martyrdom.

I have struggled with PTSD all my adult life. I sometimes find managing my daily life and its complexities challenging. However, I am gradually realizing my heavenly Father has ultimate control over everything. Even if I do not always understand His intentions for me, I have complete faith that He only desires the best for me.

Considering this, it is crucial to take on a kingdom perspective and live as though I am a mere traveler just passing through this temporary world and focusing on my ultimate destination in the heavenly realms with Christ. By doing so, I can remain grounded and centered on what truly matters and not get bogged down by the distractions and cares of this world.

Despite my imperfections, and though I often stumble, I have found encouragement in turning to God through Jesus. My adventure of discovering my true identity in Christ is ongoing. I strive each day to strengthen my relationship with God the Father with the help of the Holy Spirit. Through prayer and meditation on His Word, I look to deepen my understanding of His teachings and live a life that reflects His love and grace.

Though the road may be long and challenging, I trust in God's guidance and know He will provide me with the strength and wisdom I need to continue my spiritual race.

If you're willing to continue the path you started when you were saved and submit your life to Him, even when it doesn't seem fair, He will guide you. Just like when Jesus told Peter what would happen to him, and Peter asked about another disciple's future, Jesus replied, "What about him? You follow me."

"Jesus said this to let him know by what kind of death he would glorify God. Then Jesus told him, 'Follow me.' Peter turned around and saw behind them the disciple Jesus loved—the one who had leaned over to Jesus during supper and asked, 'Lord, who will betray you?' Peter asked Jesus, 'What about him, Lord?' Jesus replied, 'If I want him to remain alive until I return, what is that to you? As for you, follow me'" John 21:19-22 NLT.

Jesus told Peter to follow Him, but instead of responding, Peter asked about the future of another disciple. This tendency to focus on others is something we all do. We accept Jesus as our Savior, yet when He asks us to follow Him, we become preoccupied with what others are doing. We might feel that their lives are better than ours or envy someone's ministry or talents. We may think others are thriving while our lives are a mess. We might not have received the job or healing we were expecting, or we struggle to forgive those who have hurt us. The excuses are endless, and we never seem to answer Jesus' call to truly follow Him. We must follow Him on His terms, not ours. We must be willing to deny ourselves and carry our crosses; this is what faith and spiritual warfare entail.

Our heavenly Father loves us deeply and desires a daily relationship with us. He wants us to love and need Him more than our own desires. We cannot do this alone, so He is waiting and willing to help us every step of the way. We only need to ask. This invitation from Jesus, as echoed in the words of Revelation, extends to all believers:

"Behold, I stand at the door and Knock. If anyone hears my

voice and opens the door, I will come in to him and dine with him, and he with Me" Revelation 3:20.

Are you willing to take the leap and open the door to His voice? Are you prepared to take your commitment to the path of our heavenly Father to new depths? As we strive to follow Him, I'd like to share a powerful prayer from Ephesians.

"Ever since I first heard of your strong faith in the Lord Jesus and your love for God's people everywhere, I have not stopped thanking God for you. I pray for you constantly, asking God, the glorious Father of our Lord Jesus Christ, to give you spiritual wisdom and insight so that you might grow in your knowledge of God. I pray that your hearts will be flooded with light so that you can understand the confident hope he has given to those he called—his holy people who are his rich and glorious inheritance. I also pray that you will understand the incredible greatness of God's power for us who believe him. This is the same mighty power that raised Christ from the dead and seated him in the place of honor at God's right hand in the heavenly realms" Ephesians 1:15-20 NLT.

I have reworded the verse from Ephesians into a personal prayer for you. I hope it inspires and guides you, and I encourage you to pray this prayer for yourself.

Dear Lord Jesus,

I thank You for your unwavering devotion to me. Your love for me is a blessing, and I pray that You continue to grant me spiritual wisdom and insight. Please illuminate my heart with Your light so that I may understand the confident hope that You have given me. I am Your rich and glorious inheritance. Please help me grasp the tremendous power available to those who believe in You, the same awe-inspiring power that raised You from the dead and appointed You a place of honor at God's right hand in the heavenly realms. Amen.

One day, when we are with the Lord, He will be our protection—not with stone walls but a wall of fire around us, protecting us for eternity.

" 'For I,' says the LORD, 'will be a wall of fire all around her, and I will be the glory in her midst' " Zechariah 2:5.

May we all find the courage to follow our blessed Lord and seek a deeper and more intimate connection with Him. May we remain steadfast in our pursuit of His divine guidance. Let us persevere on our spiritual pilgrimage until we finally reach the gates of paradise and are reunited with Him in everlasting joy. Amen!

# REVIEW OF THE WALLS AND GATES

The wall and various gates symbolize different aspects of our spiritual journeys.

We begin with salvation through the Sheep Gate.

Then we move on to sharing our faith and growing through the Fish Gate.

We leave behind our old selves at the Old Gate.

At the Valley Gate, we focus on Jesus to overcome our trials.

The Refuse Gate helps us eliminate anything that hinders our spiritual growth.

The Fountain Gate allows the Holy Spirit to flow through us.

The Water Gate encourages us to read and practice the Word of God.

The Horse Gate teaches us to fight our battles spiritually.

We expect Jesus to return at the East Gate.

And we will stand before Him at the Inspection Gate.

I have found that following a structured outline for my personal prayer life using the walls from the book of Nehemiah helps me feel more inspired, uplifted, and organized during my prayer time. I am sharing my outline with you in the hopes that it will also be a blessing to you.

## THE SHEEP GATE - PRAYING FOR PERSONAL RESTORATION

- Reflect on your own life, acknowledging your need for restoration.
- Pray for yourself, asking for forgiveness daily, seeking renewal, healing, and strength to rebuild the walls of your own life.

## THE FISH GATE - PRAYING FOR FAMILY, COMMUNITY, AND CHURCH

- Expand your focus beyond yourself to your family, friends, church, and community.
- Offer prayers on behalf of others, asking for their salvation, well-being, guidance, and unity.

## THE OLD GATE - PRAYING FOR SPIRITUAL GROWTH AND REVELATION

- Recognize the importance of spiritual growth and a deeper relationship with our heavenly Father.
- Seek guidance from God to reveal areas where you can grow and improve in your faith journey.

## THE VALLEY GATE - PRAYING THROUGH LIFE'S CHALLENGES

- Acknowledge the valleys or challenges you are currently facing.
- Turn to God in prayer, seeking His guidance, strength, and support to overcome life's trials.

## THE REFUSE GATE - PRAYING FOR CLEANSING AND TRANSFORMATION

- Examine areas in your life that need to be cleansed or removed.
- Pray for God's help and transformation in areas where you need to let go of negativity, bad habits, or unforgiveness.

## THE FOUNTAIN GATE - PRAYING FOR THE HOLY SPIRIT'S INFILLING

- Open yourself to the Holy Spirit's presence in your life.
- Seek the Holy Spirit's guidance, wisdom, and infilling as you engage with Scripture and prayer.

## THE WATER GATE - PRAYING FOR CLARITY AND REVELATION FROM GOD'S WORD

- Approach the Word of God with a desire for deeper understanding and commitment to His Word.
- Ask God for clarity and revelation as you read, study, and meditate on His Word.

## THE HORSE GATE - PRAYING FOR SPIRITUAL WARFARE AND FAITH APPLICATION

- Acknowledge the spiritual battles you face in life.
- Seek God's help to apply His Word by faith, equipping yourself for spiritual warfare.

## THE EAST GATE - PRAYING FOR BREAKTHROUGH AND THE RETURN OF CHRIST

- Reflect on areas of your life where you need breakthrough and freedom.
- Pray for any obstacles to be removed and for the promise of Christ's return to give you hope and perspective.

## THE INSPECTION GATE - PRAYING FOR PERSONAL IMPROVEMENT AND THE FINAL JUDGMENT

- Commit to self-improvement and growth in your faith.
- Ask God for guidance in areas where you can improve and acknowledge that Jesus will, in the end, judge the living and the dead.

# MAP OF THE WALLS AND GATES

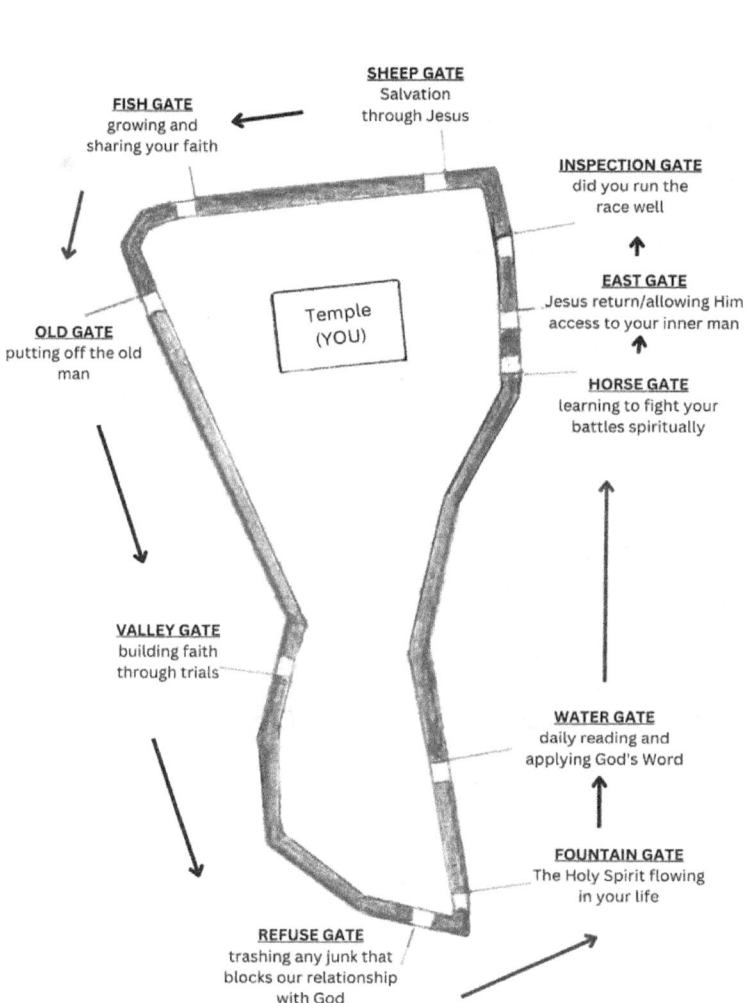

## HERE ARE JUST A FEW OF THE SCRIPTURES THAT TELL YOU WHO YOU NOW ARE IN CHRIST

I have been set free from sin (Romans 6:18).

I have peace in Christ (John 14:27).

I am not of the world (John 17:16).

I have a new life in Christ (Acts 5:20).

I have eternal life in Christ (1 John 5:11).

I have been raised to new life in Christ (Romans 6:4).

I am no longer a slave to sin (Romans 6:6).

I no longer have spiritual death but spiritual life (Romans 6:13).

I am not controlled by the flesh but by the Spirit (Romans 8:9).

I have the mind of Christ (1 Corinthians 2:16).

I'm being transformed into the likeness of Christ (2 Corinthians 3:18).

I am a new creation in Christ (2 Corinthians 5:17).

God's resurrection power is working in me (Ephesians 1:17-19).

I am seated with Christ in heavenly realms (Ephesians 2:6).

Because of Christ, sin is defeated in my life (Colossians 2:14-15).

God has given me His spirit of power, love, and wisdom (2 Timothy 1:7).

God has given me everything I need to live a godly life (2 Peter 1:3).

# ABOUT THE AUTHOR

Susan Mathis is a devoted wife, mom and grandmother whose remarkable life journey has been a testament to resilience and faith. Born into a challenging and abusive home, Susan's early years were marked by adversity and hardship. Despite these daunting circumstances, she found solace and strength in her faith, which became a guiding light in her tumultuous journey.

In her late twenties, Susan experienced a profound and life-altering moment when God brought her out of the Catholic faith, which set her on a path of self-discovery and spiritual growth.

One of the most significant challenges Susan has faced throughout her life is her battle with post-traumatic stress disorder (PTSD), a struggle that has been with her since the tender age of eight. Despite the weight of this burden, Susan's indomitable spirit and unwavering faith have propelled her forward.

In her forties, Susan felt a divine calling from God to embark on a transformative journey of personal restoration. This calling led her to delve into the profound wisdom found within the book of Nehemiah, which would serve as her guide and source of inspiration throughout her healing process.

Susan's latest work is a testament to her incredible journey of healing, growth, and transformation. Her words are a powerful reminder that even in the face of the most daunting challenges, with the power of our heavenly Father, we can overcome and flourish. Through her writing, Susan shares her story of redemption, offering hope, inspiration, and a path toward healing for those who may be walking a similar path.

With her deep-rooted faith, unwavering determination, and the wisdom she has gained from her life's trials and triumphs, Susan continues to be a source of inspiration for readers seeking strength, renewal, and a deeper connection to their own spiritual journeys.

www.ingramcontent.com/pod-product-compliance
Lightning Source LLC
Chambersburg PA
CBHW071511040426
42444CB00008B/1590